A World of Light

Portraits and Celebrations

May Sarton now and at twenty-six in a portrait by Polly Thayer

A World of Light
Portraits and Celebrations

By May Sarton

W · W · NORTON & COMPANY · INC · New York

Grateful acknowledgment is made to the following: *The New Yorker*, for permission to reprint "Marc, the Vigneron"; *Southwest Review*, for permission to reprint "Alice and Haniel Long"; *Texas Quarterly* for permission to reprint "An Informal Portrait of George Sarton"; Farrar, Straus & Giroux, Inc., for permission to print "Masked Woman's Song" and some lines from "The Dream" from Louise Bogan's *The Blue Estuaries*, copyright © 1923, 1929, 1930, 1931, 1933, 1934, 1935, 1936, 1937, 1938, 1941, 1949, 1951, 1952, 1954 by Louise Bogan.

Thanks are also due to Tony Long, Haniel Long's literary executor, for permission to print his father's and mother's letters and Haniel Long's poems; to Ruth Limmer, Louise Bogan's literary executor, for permission to print Louise Bogan's letters to the author; to Spencer Curtis Brown, Elizabeth Bowen's literary executor, for permission to print Elizabeth Bowen's letters to the author; and to the Berg Collection of the New York Public Library for permission to publish these letters as well as those of S. S. Koteliansky, all among the Sarton papers in their possession.

Published simultaneously in Canada by
Penguin Books Canada Ltd,
2801 John Street, Markham, Ontario L3R 1B4.

Printed in the United States of America.

First published as a Norton paperback 1988

Library of Congress Cataloging in Publication Data
Sarton, May, 1912–
   A world of light.
   1. Sarton, May, 1912–   —Friends and associates.
I. Title.
PS3537.A832Z526   818'.5'203 [B]   76–16796

ISBN 0-393-30500-7

3 4 5 6 7 8 9 0

FOR CAROLYN G. HEILBRUN

CONTENTS

"They are all gone into the world of light."

—Henry Vaughan

Think where man's glory most begins and ends,
And say my glory was I had such friends.

—W.B. YEATS, "The Municipal Gallery Revisited"

PREFACE

I HAVE CARRIED this book in my mind for twenty years; I wanted to fill the gap between *I Knew a Phoenix* (that ends when I was twenty-six) and *Plant Dreaming Deep* (that begins when I was forty-five) by celebrating the great friendships that flowered during those years. How does one grow? How does one change? At least in part through the influence of friends. As André Chamson has said, "A great friendship is never anything but a great inner exigency. Friends worthy of the name are always beings whose reality weighs on us with its whole weight. The only problem is not to be unequal to what they are." I have included my parents because of course their friendship has weighed on me with its full weight all my life, because, of all the influences, theirs has been the hardest to deal with, and the most inspiring.

All the people I write of are dead, except Marc, The Vigneron—all were considerably older than I. I did not consciously choose my friends among older people, but I was avid to learn and inevitably gravitated toward those who

could teach me. There are singular omissions: I have not
written, because he did not wish me to, about Basil de
Selincourt whose criticism of my poems, beginning with my
first book, were almost the only critical foundation I was
given and whose friendship was seminal. Eva Le Gallienne,
still very much alive, does not appear in this book. I have said
a very little about what she taught me in a chapter of *I
Knew a Phoenix*. And so also with Lugné-Poë, a giant of
friendship during my theatre years.

My first vision of this book was that it might resemble the
Renaissance portraits where the subject is painted with a
landscape behind him, a landscape that is very much a part
of the character and the mood of the portrait. In Part III
I have kept this concept, because in each case the person and
the place were closely intertwined. Grace Eliot Dudley did
not become her real self until she found that magic house
and garden among the vineyards of the Touraine. It became
the expression of her inner life, and so with Alice and Haniel
Long in Santa Fe, or Quig in Nelson.

Writing of these people whom I loved has been a great
deal harder than I could possibly have imagined. For nothing in the past stays fixed forever; as we grow and change the
past changes; when I looked back I did not always find
exactly what I had expected, and even such seminal friendships became mine fields. Some unexpected conflict or painful memory exploded and changed all the fixed points. This
was especially true when I was dealing with the writers,
Elizabeth Bowen and Louise Bogan. I knew Elizabeth best
when I was just beginning as a writer myself and she was at
the height of her fame, and Louise much later when I was
beginning to feel confidence in my own gifts and had published quite a lot, but had had very little recognition. These
were momentous encounters for me, but the relationship be-

tween writers is always precarious, and over a period of twenty years or more, there were bound to be tensions and/ or misunderstandings along the way. As I wrote those portraits the world of light had to suffer some admission of chiaruscuro, and I found this apprehension of reality painful.

After I had written the portraits of my parents I realized with a shock that I had not spoken at all of what it was like to be their child; I had been entirely absorbed in defining their separate essences. Again I have come to understand some things only now, many years after their deaths, my mother's in 1950 and my father's six years later. And it is not so much what I remember as things I cannot remember but have pondered on that have yielded up startling truths and have helped me to understand myself.

During the first two years of my life in the small heaven of our house in Wondelgem, Belgium, I was snatched away from my mother for weeks at a time because of her illnesses, sent to stay with friends, or, for one period of more than a month, given into the care of a dear friend who came to Wondelgem to look after me. When I was two we were driven out by the war, and again I was sent to cousins in England while my mother and father tried to find a means of livelihood in London. What all these uprootings did, I think, was to make the baby and small child learn to put out roots very quickly for survival. I became passionately attached to whoever took care of me, and perhaps this explains what someone called "emotional facility" when I was grown up. We were not able to settle anywhere for the first six years of my life. Then at last we reached Cambridge, Massachusetts, where my parents stayed for good, which became home; even so, we moved every seven years when my father had a sabbatical and we all went to Europe, the furniture being put in storage and a new apartment found on our return. It is not surprising, then, that I have always felt nostalgia for families rooted in one place, for the rites and routines of "family life."

My parents were remarkable, since I was an only child, in always leaving me free to do what I wanted and to be myself. My mother's theory of education was to be quite severe when I was an infant and until I was about ten years old, and then to give me almost absolute freedom of choice. As a child I left the house for the Shady Hill School at about seven every morning on my bicycle and came home often after dark. No one ever said, "Don't climb that tree; you might fall." When I wanted to go to camp, my mother made it possible for me to do so; I spent summers or parts of summers with the families of school friends—the Hockings in Vermont, the Runkles in Duxbury, Massachusetts, the Copley Greenes at Rowley, Massachusetts, the Boutons at Kearsage, New Hampshire. After I graduated from high school I had only one dream—to enter Eva Le Gallienne's Civic Repertory Theatre in New York. It was not easy, especially for my father, to accept the idea of a perilous life in the theatre in lieu of four years at Vassar. He battled it out with me for months before he consented, and then agreed to one hundred dollars a month allowance. My mother went to New York and found a club where I could stay near the theatre, where I would have some protection. How marvelous it was of them both to back me as they did with both moral and financial support when the whole precarious plan must have created great anxiety! There are few holidays in the theatre and sometimes I did not get home for months. So I had really left the nest for good at the remarkably early age of seventeen.

My father had never been a father in the usual sense. He could not, absorbed as he was almost totally in his work, really pay attention, and when I was small I learned to be very silent, for he worked at home and the slightest noise interrupted his concentration. So at an early age I witnessed the fact that work was of the first importance, and that it justified rather inhuman behavior. I don't know when I began to be aware of the rifts in the marriage, but certainly before I was ten. My father, for instance, hated Christmas. (It was not in the Belgian tradition, where presents are given on St. Nicholas on the 6th of December.) We always had a small tree and my mother stayed up late making marvelous clothes for my dolls. One Christmas Eve I heard from my bed my father's rage at what he said was "spoiling May" and my mother's sobs. I woke the next day, Christmas day, with a high fever. That was a dramatic instance of his lack of sensitivity (also perhaps unconscious jealousy, for he had lost his own mother when he had been a baby and nobody "spoiled" him); but every Christmas was a time of strain because of his feelings about it. So, in the usual sense of the word, we did not have a family life. I had to grow up before I could understand that he himself was a child who never grew up in the emotional areas of his being. He usually gave me for my birthday a book that he wanted—for instance, when I was eleven and could have had no possible interest in it, an expensive French-English, English-French two-volume dictionary, which then of course disappeared into his own library! I found it there after his death, and it came in very handy when I was translating Valéry with Louise Bogan.

Because of his need to concentrate absolutely on his work George Sarton had developed extreme resistance to anything that might prove disturbing, such as my mother's health or lack of it, or any need I might have that would require painful discussion. It is amazing, since both my mother and I suffered because of this, that I never resented that work, any more than she did. We honored him for it, and never doubted that, whatever the cost, we were contributing to something of real importance. It was George Sarton's example as a scholar not as a human being that molded me. I did not come to love him as a human being until after my mother's death, when I myself was middle-aged.

But what my father represented was in extreme contrast to what my mother expected of herself and of me in human terms. I thought of her always as my dearest friend, an equal, *the* person with whom I could discuss anything and everything—my passions, my admirations, my griefs, my discoveries, my torments. She backed me to the limit, but she was also my best critic, with an unerring eye for self-dramatization or any false attitude. She was simply inside my life, as my father was simply outside it. And for her, especially in the later years, I was also the best friend, the one who could understand and share.

She had married an extraordinary man who loved her deeply, as she loved him. Never did either of them look at any other person with such love as they gave each other. But she had also married an emotional cripple, unable ever to discuss money (of which there was always too little) and fleeing any emergency that might require real self-giving on his part.

My mother never made scenes. She buried her anger, because, however angry she was—and with reason—she still felt that George Sarton must be protected, never upset by any demands of hers, for the sake of his work. The cost was high, high in ill health, migraine, and I have sometimes wondered whether the cancer of which she died might not have been caused by buried rage. And the cost was high for me because I suffered for and with her, yet could do nothing. But of course I learned from all this, and slowly learned to love my father (as she had done) for what he was, and to forget what he could not be.

On less emotional levels we were a trio who enjoyed each

other immensely and who were quite independent of each other, for we all had consuming interests of our own. I began to write poetry when I was ten or eleven; my mother had her own inventive ways of teaching and her own work. When we met at meals there was always passionate discussion of books and art. And I have wonderful memories of summers we spent together in Ogunquit, and one memorable journey for a summer in the Pyrenees after my mother and I had spent a hard winter in Belgium. That journey has kept its dreamlike happiness for nearly fifty years. Our slow progress from one mountain village to another, where we took long walks, and I collected wild flowers to press . . . the vivid rural scenes—once we came upon a sheepshearing, and I watched with amazement the thick golden fleece gradually being clipped by hand and rolled over in a great rich furl . . . the awesome Cirque de Gavarnie . . . and especially my curiosity about the Basque people, which drove me to read all I could about them. But most of all what keeps its glow was the fact that we were happy that summer, all three.

Being the child of George and Mabel Sarton was an intense experience and an immensely rich one as I look back on it now. It was a rich experience to grow up between two such powerful personalities and to absorb their values, little by little.

Through my father I witnessed that if the vision were there, a man could work eighteen hours a day, with joy, and never seem to tire. I understood that a talent is something given, that it opens like a flower, but without exceptional energy, discipline, and persistence will never bear fruit.

Through my mother I witnessed extreme awareness of all forms of beauty, and extreme sensitivity to human beings and human relationships. Mother, wife, friend, as well as artist—she had to balance a thousand things into a complex whole, and often felt torn among them. I see her as giving a little more than she could afford in every direction; the demands she made on herself were enormous.

And quite early on I began to experience the conflict implied in an effort to be as human as my mother and as dedicated as my father, for these two qualities are often in opposition. Though not always. My father, like me, answered every letter—that was his way of being human. I always knew that I had a responsibility toward life itself to do something in my own right, to contribute, to create. That was simply taken for granted in the ethos in which I grew up.

But an historian can believe that his work is bound to be of value if he goes to primary sources, and is diligent and perceptive. No writer can have that assurance, filled as he is with the same anxiety and doubt during the creation of each new work. The work of an historian is cumulative; for the artist each new work is the rival of all that has gone before. And beyond even self-doubt no writer can justify ruthlessness for the sake of his work, because being human to the fullest possible extent is what his work demands of him. The conflict between life and art is bound to be acute and the finding of a balance an excruciating daily struggle, the more so for me because I had before me such extreme examples of each mode in my remarkable parents.

Both had died before I was forty-five. The imprint was deep, and I realized its depth partly because I felt great relief. When my mother died I felt relief for her (it had been a long hard death from cancer), and relief for myself because I knew that the worst thing that could ever happen to me had happened. Never again would I wake up in tears from the nightmare that she had died. Only my own death would ever take from me as much. My father bore his loss

with great dignity and courage, and in the six years before
he himself died suddenly of a heart attack, I came to know
and to love him in a new way. But when they were both
gone, I felt freed of a great burden, the burden of being a
child. I felt free to be wholly myself, especially as a writer.
I could not, I think, have come out as I did in *Mrs. Stevens
Hears the Mermaids Singing* while they were alive. I also
felt a new responsibility, since a person without any family
can afford to be honest in a way that perhaps no one with
any close ties can be.

But I miss my parents, the more lately as the world
around us darkens and there seems so little foundation of
belief on which to stand. I long to run over to Channing
Place for tea, to find my mother lying on the chaise longue
in the garden, a cat on her lap, my father smoking a cigar
in a chair beside her—the two people in the world with
whom I could feel in total communion about politics, art,
religion, all that really matters, to be reassured by their un-
failing and concerned idealism, and to laugh again as we
three often laughed together at this "preposterous pig of a
world." Without them I sometimes feel the wind at my back
—they had such vitality and strength.

When I was thirty I once said to my mother, "If I died
now, I would feel that I had lived an extraordinary life . . ."
I meant as a human being, not as an artist. I was acknowledg-
ing that I had already then been given the friendship and
love of many different people, people as rare and precious as
stars, people whom I had watched and learned from and admired with the intensity of an astronomer discovering a new
brilliant in the heavens. In ten years I had experienced a
great flowering inside myself, a flowering, not a harvest, for
it had had that poignance of a long-delayed spring, almost
too much happening too quickly, and not to be held fast,

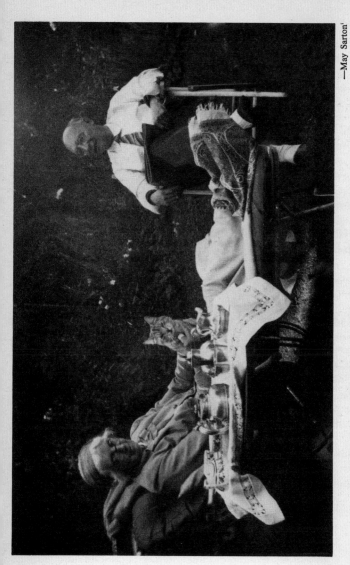

—May Sarton[1]

Mabel and George Sarton in the garden at Channing Place

only adored for a moment, and let go. Fulfillment would come much later, and in solitude.

Almost all of those celebrated here had come into my ken before I was forty, and although they are now dead, I am constantly aware of their presence. During the months of the writing it has been almost overwhelming—overwhelming because I have been increasingly aware of the past as flux, changing as we change even from day to day, changing as the sea changes under the influences of sky, wind, and the moon. How to pin down even a small part of the truth? It is so elusive. How to deal with such complexity in such a small space? How to find the balance between the essence of a person and our relationship?

Every day I make some gesture, think or feel something through the influence of one or another of these friends. When I plant bulbs I pat the earth around each one and realize suddenly that that is what my mother did; I never cook carrots without remembering thyme, a little onion, and sugar as Céline used to do, or make my bed without a vivid recalling of Grace Dudley's insistence on hospital corners as we stretched a sheet taut between us; when I take my father's cane on a walk with my dog I find myself striding along as briskly as he did; on the rare occasions when I drink a martini the image wells up of the square cut-glass bottle with buffalo grass in it from which Kot poured gin for James Stephens and me; I see the reds among the fresh greens of spring with Quig's eyes. These are not conscious evocations nor very important in themselves, but it is their interweaving through every day that explains what influence truly is. We become what we have loved.

At the end of writing a book I suspect that every writer feels impoverishment, the impoverishment of knowing he has expressed inadequately what he had wished to communicate, as well as a sense of loss because it has gone from him. "But who," I am reminded by Freya Stark, "has not for some wild moments thought to recall the irrecoverable with words?"

                                                    May Sarton

York, Maine
November, 1975

Part I

George Sarton

ONE

An Informal Portrait of George Sarton

MANY YEARS AFTER my father's death I received a letter from a stranger who had just discovered George Sarton, one of those moving readers who comes upon a classic work, ignorant, as it were, and under his own steam, with the freshness of personal adventure: "I can only say that your father's great work moves me just as does the final fugue in The Art of the Fugue where Bach sums up all musical knowledge in a quadruple—and also unfinished—fugue." My correspondent had just discovered the two-volume *History of Science* —"an unfinished fugue," since those on Greek and Hellenistic science would have been followed by other volumes through the Middle Ages and into the Renaissance if George Sarton had lived longer.

"What manner of man was he?" the letter concludes. "I

shall not cease to wonder about this marvelous genius who said, 'Erudition without pedantry is as rare as wisdom itself,' and then wrote 1,200 pages of erudition without any trace of pedantry. . . ." This sketch of George Sarton is a belated answer to that letter.

What manner of man was he? He was an exceedingly charming man; this charm made itself felt at once, on first meeting, in his beaming smile, the smile of a delighted and sometimes mischievous child that flashed out below the great domed forehead and sensitive brown eyes behind their thick glasses. He was stout, with beautiful hands and small feet, a stocky man who walked down Brattle Street in Cambridge, Massachusetts, at exactly the same time every morning, with the propulsive energy of a small steam engine, a French beret on his head, a briefcase in one hand, in a coat a little too long for him because he could not be bothered to have his clothes altered and insisted on buying them off a rack to save time.

What manner of man was he who moved with extraordinary freedom over the ages and the continents within a daily orbit as undeviating as that of any planet? A man of disciplined routine yet who lived surrounded by what might be called the communion of saints: "Today is the first day of spring," he notes in his journal, "the feast of St. Benedict (the beginning of the Middle Ages) and Bach's birthday— what a conjunction!" A man bent over a desk in a tiny book-filled study in the Widener Library at Harvard University for many hours each day, whose image of himself was that of a crusader in a holy war—the war to convince the universities and the academies that the history of science must be treated as a separate discipline, and the war to convince the public at large that the history of science could be a saving grace.

A man who at one time chose to spend his Saturday afternoons at the Museum of Fine Arts in Boston, studying Chinese painting for the sheer pleasure of it. "Who is that man who must be a specialist since he comes so regularly and studies so hard?" someone asked. "Oh, that is George Sarton, the historian of science, taking a half day's holiday," came the startling answer.

A young Belgian who, having just founded the first international journal for the history of science, suddenly found himself transported, with his English wife and baby daughter, to a strange country across the seas; who translated himself into a new tongue when he was over thirty; and who, at over forty, decided that he would have to learn Arabic for the sake of his medieval studies, did so, and read the whole of *Arabian Nights* in the original tongue with huge enjoyment. The least self-aware man who ever kept a journal, the most innocent and willful of hearts, who could seem totally unaware of the inner lives of those close to him, yet who enacted within himself a daily drama of self-criticism and heroic endeavor—above all, a scholar in the old-fashioned sense of the word, a dedicated man, a man of endless ardor and curiosity, one of the great pioneers in a new discipline.

As one way of trying to answer the question "What manner of man was George Sarton?" let us follow him through a specimen day. We have watched his elated progress down Brattle Street; after his death several neighbors mentioned their delight in seeing him go past each morning like some Twentieth Century Express with a destination five centuries back in time, perhaps, at a station called Athens or Rome or Mecca or Constantinople or Peking—toward Widener 189 where the five volumes of *An Introduction to the History of Science* were slowly being delved out and written.

The glass door of Widener 189 bore the inscription ISIS; not a reference (as at least one person imagined it might be)

to a collection of Gertrude Steiniana, nor an assertion of Being, but the title of the quarterly George Sarton founded
and edited for more than forty years. Once he had locked
himself safely behind that door, the first thing he did each
morning, of course, was to run through the mail, which
might bring him letters and queries from scholars and friends
in England, Japan, Arabia, Israel, France, Russia—in this
sense alone he was truly "a man of the world," a man of
many letters, a man of few if any intimate friends except
epistolary ones. So it happened that in 1953 I picked up a
dictionary of current American slang translated into Japanese by Professor Shituka Saito and discovered that it had
been inscribed "To Professor Doctor George Sarton, my best
friend." When I inquired who this unknown intimate was,
my father gave me one of his slightly guilty yet innocent
smiles and answered, "I have never seen him, as a matter
of fact." Yet I am sure that Professor Saito was being a
little more than polite, and it is quite possible that he had
been the recipient of several of those outbursts of rage or
self-pity or mere self-revelation that took the place with
George Sarton of intimacy in the ordinary sense.

In the morning's mail there would be the usual pile of
books and periodicals, and, every now and then, a twenty-
pound sack of birdseed as well. George Sarton loved to feed
the pigeons who came to coo at the windowsill, and even
nested there, so that the endless writing in that fine hand was
accompanied by the raising of innumerable pigeon families
within two feet of his left elbow. Unfortunately professors
and students who had offices across the court did not enjoy
the sight of such untidiness in the sacred precincts. Reports
reached the authorities, and George Sarton was requested
to desist. This was the occasion of a notable exchange of
letters, the opening shot being Sarton's expression of horror
that Widener would consider becoming a second-class li-

brary, since every first-class library the world over, including the British Museum, had its pigeons. And for a time there was a truce. But the cleaning of the court was becoming a real problem, and after some months George Sarton surrendered in a final subdued letter in which he granted that if he had to choose between offending his neighbors and offending the pigeons, he supposed his neighbors must come first. I don't imagine that even kind Dr. Metcalf, then head of the Widener Library, had any idea of the inner agitation with which my father denied the pleading and sometimes even aggressively irritated pecks at his window for some months before the pigeons too gave up. Perhaps they eventually found their way, as did the sacks of seed, to his house in Channing Place, and thus set their seal of pigeonly approval on a remarkable personal library.

The mail attended to, George Sarton could finally get to work. On Columbus Day of 1942 he noted in his journal, "The difficulty—as well as the delight—of my work lies in its great diversity. There is much unity of single-mindedness deep in it—but the surface is infinitely diversified. For example, last Saturday I was revising completely my notes on the Persian theologian Al-Tăftăzani. Yesterday and today I had to prepare four lectures to be given tomorrow and Wednesday—dealing respectively with

1) The history of science in general (Colby)
2) Science and religion
3) The Western discovery of printing (Radcliffe)
4) Leonardo da Vinci, man of science (American Academy) (Radcliffe)."

We cannot watch a mind at work. We can only measure its caliber by the results. The five monumental volumes called *An Introduction to the History of Science* did not go farther than the fourteenth century. But, to give a specific idea of the

breadth of the man, as well as of his concentrated power, consider that after his retirement from teaching at sixty-five, he
published four books—*Ancient Science and Modern Civili-
zation* (The Montgomery Lectures, University of Nebraska
Press, 1954); *Galen of Pergamon* (The Logan Clandening
Lectures on the History and Philosophy of Science, University of Kansas Press, 1954); *The Appreciation of Ancient and
Medieval Science during The Renaissance* (1450–1600)
(University of Pennsylvania Press, 1955); *Six Wings, Men
of Science in the Renaissance*, (The Patten Foundation Lectures, University of Indiana Press, 1957)—and that during
this time he was also working on the two huge volumes on
Greek and Hellenistic science to which I have already referred, the last of which appeared posthumously, but had
been completed before his death.

The days at the office, even when he was not lecturing,
were tense and packed. Then, at about four o'clock (though
in the later years he sometimes went home at lunchtime),
he walked back the full mile to Channing Place, carrying
as likely as not two briefcases stuffed with books and papers.
There he would be welcomed by my mother and Cloudy,
the gray Persian cat, her plume of a tail in air, and soon all
three settled down for their ritual tea in the big living room
or, from June to October, out-of-doors in the garden. It was
the time of intimate exchanges, the relation to each other of
the day's accomplishments and difficulties, and the impas-
sioned discussions on art and life which made this marriage
such a continuously alive one. He might have brought her
an art book from Widener, producing it from his briefcase
with the air of a magician; for there were many lacunae in
his usefulness to the household, but he would always gladly
search out and carry home a heavy book!

George Sarton, who had grown up in a bourgeois society
where women were indulged rather than respected, emerged

as a young man into the artistic and social ferment of the
city of Ghent at the turn of the century, and became an ardent feminist and socialist; several of his friends among
women were artists, including his future wife (as in his later
years at least three of his women friends were distinguished
scholars); he always had respect for women's judgment and
gifts. My mother was not a learned person, but she was an
artist and had a spirit that matched his in its intensity, although since her life was twice dislocated by transplanting,
first from England to Belgium, and then from Belgium to the
United States, her gifts had to be turned primarily to help
us keep afloat financially, and so perhaps never fully flowered. But that these two shared a true companionship about
all the things that mattered most to them (including cats
and gardens!) is clear. I was delighted to find the following
note in my father's journals: "A flower garden is a poetic
creation. Any woman who knows how to grow flowers and
loves them is immensely superior to one who does not." My
happiest vision of these parents of mine is of my mother lying in the garden at teatime on a chaise longue, a white
shawl flung rather elegantly round her shoulders, a cat on
her lap, looking at her husband with a slightly quizzical
tender expression, and of my father, a battered soft straw hat
tilted down over his eyes, smoking a cigar and enjoying her
creation, the garden: I sometimes think this hour was the
only relaxed one of his day. The journal notes more than
once, "A Blessed day—thanks as always to Mabel."

Of course she mothered him, and I think he was quite
unaware of it, although he often called her "Mother," as he
had done since I was a child; he was chiefly aware of his
very real deprivation in his own infancy and while he was
growing up, and there are several references to it in the
journal. Among these, one seems to me especially characteristic in its approach to an intimate matter; it was written on

his sixty-second birthday: "I have now discovered that the
thirty-first of August is the saint's day of the Spaniard Raymond Nonnatus (1200–1240). He was called Non-natus because he was 'not-born,' but removed from his mother's
womb after her death. My own fate was not very different
from his, because my mother died soon after my birth and I
never knew her. Neither did I really miss her until I saw
Mabel mothering our child. Then only could I measure the
greatness of my loss. Many of my shortcomings are due to
the fact that I had no mother, and that my good father had
no time to bother much about me. I am indeed 'an unlicked
bear' (*un ours mal lèché*)."

I must append to this passage one from a later entry on
the same subject, this one written after my mother's death,
"I sometimes mutter, 'Bear it, Bear!' or else 'Five Bears!'
which is an abbreviated form of the great rule of conduct
'Bear and Forbear.'" Bear and forbear he did, even when
a pipe burst, the cellar flooded, and his response was "Let
nature take its course," as he went upstairs to his study, leaving my mother to cope! You who ask, "What manner of man
was he?" Was he not a charming man? Whatever his faults
as a human being, whatever his lacks as husband and father
(they were not inconsiderable), all must be forgiven such innocence and such charm.

But by now tea is over, and George Sarton has disappeared into the upper regions of the house, to his study there,
with its shelves and shelves of records and books, and its
pigeon-frequented balcony. There, as he himself explains,
"For the last twenty or thirty years it has been my habit to
spend at least a half hour before dinner reading Arabic,
Greek or Latin (not Hebrew, my knowledge of it being in-
sufficient) and that reading, which is necessarily *slow* (even
in Arabic) is restful. It is like praying, for it implies a hum-

bler and quieter state of mind." As long as my mother was alive, this period of quiet reading was followed by an hour or so of recorded music. Methodical in all things, George Sarton always noted what records he had played in every month. In April of 1952, for instance, I find that he had been listening to Dvořak, Gluck, Beethoven, Brahms, Palestrina, Stravinsky, Chopin, Pergolesi. Curiosity and a developing musical taste led him to buy many recordings of modern music, some of which he came to enjoy (it was he who introduced me to Mahler), but in 1952 he explodes in his journal, "Many modern composers make me think of people who cannot tell a joke without punching you in the back; they are so brutal, they insist with increasing noise. I am willing to forget their dissonances and I would gladly smile or laugh if they were not so terribly anxious. They seem to say: 'You have never heard music like this' and they deafen you. Impudent rascals.

"Yet if I must choose between artistic impudence on the one hand and administrative complacency and stupidity on the other, I shall never hesitate—give me the impudent artists and the rebels."

There speaks my father, who had observed Parkinson's Law long before Mr. Parkinson did. In 1954 he was writing in his journal, "The steady development of administration everywhere afflicts me more than I can say because it always implies irreversible losses in personality and humanity. It is now spreading with the virulence and malignity of a cancer. It does not affect only offices (like the Postal one, the Treasury, etc.) but universities, museums, and many scholars and artists today have the mentality of an administrator if not of a business man. Think of a university Professor who manages his work and thinks steadily of his 'interests' in the same spirit as the owner of a delicatessen store. I know such. What caused that pitiful disease? Is it the result of the growth of

industry and technology, of the availability of more machines
and gadgets, or is it simply the result of growing numbers
of people? Every administration grows like a cancer. Administrative problems grow much faster than the number of
students and teachers. . . ." and he adds in a typical perora-
tion, "It is high time for me to leave this mechanical and administrative world and return to the bosom of Nature."

Possibly the violence of this reaction became a crotchet
in the later years; or perhaps it was rather a kind of passive
resistance, the involuted answer to certain real humiliations
which he had suffered during World War II when, for instance, the then head of the Carnegie Institution (which, it
must also be remembered, had generously supported my
father through the years) told him to his face that the history
of science had become "irrelevant." For George Sarton and
his way of thinking, the history of science and its humaniz-
ing influence would never be less "irrelevant" than in an age
of vast technological progress, and never less "irrelevant"
than in time of war, if the values for which we fought were
to be preserved. But whatever the subconscious reasons may
have been, it must be admitted that my father was the "en-
fant terrible" of administrators, and at one time threw away
letters from the Harvard deans without opening them, as
"irrelevant"; if this was childishness, and it surely was, the
childishness sprang from a kernel of hard-won personal truth.

When George Sarton first came to Harvard through the
kind offices of L. J. Henderson, he had no official position in
the university; a viva voce arrangement was made with President Lowell that he teach a half-course in the history of
science in exchange for a study at the Widener Library. It
must be remembered that he was already a fellow of the Carnegie Institution and was receiving a modest stipend from
them. No doubt from President Lowell's point of view it had
seemed a fair arrangement. But when, after twenty years,

this informal agreement had added up to an enormous amount of work without pay, or ridiculously low pay, George Sarton, too shy or too proud to complain, had taken a stance of bitter resentment against Harvard.

The incoming President Conant made all possible amends within his power—the modest lecturer was given a Professorship and an Honorary Doctorate. But the tragic flaw in George Sarton's relations with the university remained, and the wound was never healed. However, his relations with the staff at the Widener Library, to whom he owed much, were cordial and even affectionate: "I do not love Harvard so much, a hard stepmother, but I love the library, and I am grateful to all its officers, from the top Dr. Metcalf, to the girls who replace books on the shelves."

There is no doubt that George Sarton's image of himself as a kind of martyr was somewhat unrealistic, but was it not a concomitant part of the fury with which he set himself to work? He studied as other men have gone to war; the sense of a great mission was constant, and alas, great passion is inevitably flawed. For those who inherit a wilderness the pioneers have opened up and civilized for them, certain graces are possible which were denied their forbears.

I was the more touched to find in one of the journal entries in the last year of George Sarton's life a belated recognition that, after all, fate had been kind. Here he gently lays aside the mantle of isolation and injustice which he had worn with such dramatic verve for so long. The entry is called "Conversation with Rufus" (Rufus was his orange cat): "As I was going down from my study I passed Mabel's bedroom and found Rufus stretched out luxuriously on her bed. His red fur was shining in the sun, and he looked very handsome. I stroked him and said, 'You are a very happy puss. To think that you came here as a beggar, sitting at the threshold, without any introduction or explanation. You were taken in, and now you enjoy all the comforts of a big house, garden and wood. . . . You are a lucky puss.'

"He opened wide his big eyes, looked at me without smiling, and finally answered (this was the first time I heard him speak and I was taken aback), 'You are a good master and I love you as much as I can, but speaking of luck, what about yours? If the Carnegie Institution had not come to your rescue what would have happened? You would have been finished.'

"Puss was right. Every creature needs luck, and he is very ungrateful who ascribes his success to his merit and naught else. All the merit in the world will not save a man against bad luck. The theory of success is written by successful men who would be wiser if they boasted less. . . ."

These journal entries were written at the end of the day after supper, when my father returned eagerly to his study to get back to what he called "lazy work": "The best time of every day is the evening. A simple meal, a glass of wine, half an hour of music and then lazy work. That is my best working time: creative laziness."

His idea of "lazy work" would have seemed like labor to most of us, for it was in the long evenings when he sat in his big chair, smoking a pipe, his feet (so small in their soft slippers) stretched out on a pouf, a pad and pencils at his elbow, that he kept up the critical bibliographies so valuable to historians of science. What exactly did this mean? It meant reading or at least scanning all the books in the field as they came out, and making a critical note describing their contents, these notes to be collated periodically in *Isis*. In 1952, when it became necessary to cut down somewhere, this was the logical place, and at that time the journal notes: "Sunday, 5203.23 Laetare. The preparation of these 79 bibliographies represents an almost uninterrupted labor of forty-one years (beginning in 1912 to the end of 1952). If we assume that the 79 C.B. include 100,000 notes, this means that I have written an average of *six* notes a day (holidays included).

"It is like the walking of 1,000 miles in 1,000 consecutive hours. To write six notes each day for a few days is nothing, but to do so without stop or weakness for 14,975 days is an achievement. It implies at least some constancy!"

When, finally, he had spent an hour or two at his "lazy work," the time had come to assess the day. "It has been my habit for a great many years (some thirty?) to unite two numbers in my pocket diary. The first is the number of hours of work, the second (varying from 1 to 5) indicating my state of happiness or grace." Dear methodical man! I have an idea that if the state of grace was as high as 5, he then rewarded himself with a good cigar and some reading purely for enjoyment. He was always discovering writers for himself—George Eliot, for instance (as a boy of course he had missed the English classics, as he was reading the French ones), or Turgenev, or Freya Stark; sometimes he re-read an old favorite such as Geoffrey Scott's *Portrait of Zélide*, and every week he read *The New Yorker* with absorbed interest. So the long rich day came to an end and George Sarton went down the two flights to call Rufus in, lock the door, and go to bed, where, as he often said, he "slept like a log."

Does the figure of a man begin to emerge from these pages, the style of a man, the being of a man?

The concentrated essence emerges from a sampling of journal entries from 1945 to 1953—a little bouquet of humors, beliefs, self-analyses, and pleasures as I came upon them the other day scattered through the thick black spring binders where the journal was kept on lined loose-leaf paper. It will be remembered that each entry was preceded by the name of the Saint's Day. George Sarton was not a Catholic;

in his family the men were anti-Catholic and the women, on
the whole, Catholic. His father, for instance, was a high
officer in the Masonic Order, but his father's sister Elisa
(Mère Marie d'Agréda) became Mother Superior in the So-
ciété de Marie-Réparatrice, and was wholeheartedly respected and admired by her nephew George. Beyond this
personal reason, why did he always keep such tender respect
for the Church? I have an idea that it was in part historical
piety, his sense of the continuity of the spirit of man, his
wish to feel himself surrounded by all these unworldly souls,
the communion of saints on earth; it is a fact that the only
reading he abhorred was in metaphysics. He was truly religious in spirit, but he was not interested in metaphysical
speculations, and found even Plato irritating. A friend once
found him in a mood of despair in his little study at Widener,
where he ejaculated in a tone of exasperated misery, "My
wife is dying and I have had to read Plato all morning!" He
would have been hard to "convert"; he remained a liberal
in politics all his life, and the worldly and political aspects
of the Church (where clerical administrators lurk) would
have been unacceptable to his uncompromising stance.

Here, then, is the man talking to himself:

[HE ALWAYS DATED LETTERS AND JOURNAL ENTRIES BY A
METHOD OF HIS OWN INVENTION. THE FIRST TWO NUMERALS
REFER TO THE YEAR, THE SECOND TWO TO THE MONTH, AND
THE FINAL TWO TO THE DAY OF THE MONTH.]

Friday, 4506.08
Cloudy's Death . . . Cloudy, alias "Big Puss," was a
Persian cat who had shared our lives in Channing Place
since 1932. She was thus in her 14th year and had given
us a hundred kittens. We miss her. She was so beautiful
and sweet. If there is a heaven for cats she is there now . . .
Adieu, sweet Puss!

4508.28

Bless the crickets that chirp all night, when the birds are not singing.

The hotter it is and the louder they chirp. I can *hear* how hot it is. There are simpler ways, however, of measuring the temperature.

4511.17 St. Gregory Thaumaturgos

We cannot reach God except through our fellowmen. We cannot really love him except in them. We can do nothing for him except through them, and whatever good or evil we do to them we do to him. Nothing can be clearer, or more certain to me, than that.

4511.25

The first time I saw my whole head in a mirror was thirty years ago when I was lecturing at the University of Illinois in Urbana. The bathroom of the house where I was staying contained a triple mirror (like an open triangle) and I suddenly saw my head sidewise, and did not like it. In fact, I was shocked.

In recent times I have often interrogated my mirror, and not only when I was shaving. I caught myself doing so, and tried to understand why I did it.

The reason was not difficult to discover. I often feel very tired, and I am asking the mirror, "Do I look as tired as I feel?" The answer is sometimes *yes*, sometimes *no*,— for I feel too tired for expression.

4708.31 Sixty Third Birthday

This birthday ended the hardest summer of my life— hard labor on the index to Vol. III. I began the preparation of the main index on 4707.07 and ended 4708.15. Greek Index 4707.12–18; Chinese index 4708.15–26; Japanese Index 4707.27–29. The main index was ended and

the Chinese one begun on The Assumption—the most
memorable Assumption of my life next to the one in 1925
when Mabel, May and I were in Lourdes, in the Pyrenees.

Hard as it was, the work was bearable because I
thought of its usefulness, and because I realized that this
was the last large (gigantic) index of my life. An index
is the nearest approach in the world of scholarship to char-
ity in common life. Whether this was due to accumulated
tiredness and the need of relaxation, or simply to a kind
of hay-fever, this birthday found me somewhat depressed
and deflated.

4709.04

This morning, having finished all urgent work, I left
at about eleven for a halfday holyday in Boston (the first
since June 18th, almost three months ago). I went to the
Museum of Fine Arts where I lunched, then in the afternoon to the Exeter to see two English films, neither very
good, but I was in the mood to be entertained. Then I
walked to the Public Gardens where I spent a delightful
half hour watching the ducks, swans, pigeons, squirrels,
and the people. Then home where I found Mabel—a
lovely day.

St. Thomas of Villanova 4709.22

The pigeons and other birds in the garden give me
great pleasure. They sit on the balustrade of the balcony
and watch me working in my study; they must think of
me as the old man in a cage, for they are free while I seem
to be confined. My only objection to them is that they
do not allow the other birds to share the meals which I
provide for them, except the small part which they throw
overboard in their eagerness. . . .

I wish there were a pond close to the house and that

we could give hospitality to wild ducks and swans, but one cannot have everything, and I am well satisfied with the pigeons, starlings, chickadees, blue birds, etc., and with the squirrels. We sometimes hear an owl at night but never saw him.

St. Nicolas 4712.06

[THE ENTRY IS A LONG ONE ABOUT OUR GOOD-BYES TO THE NURSE COMPANION OF NEIGHBORS OF OURS, WHO BECAME MORTALLY ILL AND DECIDED TO GO HOME TO NORWAY TO DIE. THE PASSAGE ABOUT THIS TRAGIC LEAVE-TAKING ENDS, "THE SAILING AWAY OF A PERSON TO GO AND DIE IN A FOREIGN COUNTRY ACROSS THE OCEAN."

This made a deep impression upon me and yet I am ashamed to confess that my attention was soon diverted by a series of petty accidents. Doctor Ayer wrote me that there might be sugar in my urine and that a new examination was necessary. The only pair of trousers I had left contained many holes; it was clearly going to pieces. I broke my only watch, and am now a timeless man. Professor Ware communicated new difficulties concerning the printing of the Chinese index. I discovered the need of preparing a few more lectures to complete my course on ancient science. . . .

5204.28

I have always envied the good orthodox people and have always been heterodox; I could not help it. Nobody can help being what he is. I might say that I have tried all my life to be orthodox, "bien pensant," and have never quite succeeded.

5210.28

What a conjunction of major stars in 1685, Handel born in Halle, Saxony; Bach in Eisenbach; Domenico Scarlatti in Naples. They died in the fifties of the next century. . . .

5302.04

It is curious how some of our common names are badly, stupidly chosen. For example one speaks of the golden age as being in the remote past. That "golden" age was an age of relative poverty. Why call it "golden"? As soon as the gold began to flow in, everything became tawdry and cheap. Instead of "golden age" we should call it the age of poverty and innocence, the age of virtue.

5303.28 St. Giovanni da Capistrano (1385–1456)

I am deeply interested in the saints because they are rebels against material comfort and money, defenders of the spiritual life. They are the heroes of the human conscience, but my interest is not restricted to the Christian saints, and on the other hand, I realize that in early days canonizations were often arbitrary. Take the case of Isadore of Seville, a great name in the history of the Spanish Church and in the history of medieval science.

Let us assume he was a real saint; the Church did not canonize him alone however; but also his brothers Leander and Fulgentuis and his sister Florentina. Hence four brothers and sisters were saints. Is that credible? At any rate, it must have been a unique conjunction. It is very probable that the greatest saints have never been discovered; their sainthood was too deep to be obvious.

The pope ought to canonize the unknown saint.

5310.19 St. Frideswide

It is a great pleasure to sit either alone or with friends in my little dining room. During my travels I sometimes thought that I would never see it again.

When I am alone I see St. Jerome in front of me, and to my left Kobo Daishi. They represent two different worlds, two ages, and two periods in my own development. St. Jerome and Kobo, have they ever come together anywhere but in Channing Place?"

[THE ST. JEROME WAS A LARGE REPRODUCTION OF EL GRECO'S PAINTING; IT WAS THE ONE THING MY FATHER'S FAITHFUL HOUSEKEEPER, JULIA, ASKED TO HAVE WHEN THE HOUSE WAS BROKEN UP. THE PORTRAIT OF KOBO DAISHI AS A CHILD, A REPRODUCTION OF A PAINTING BY NOBUZANE (1177–1265) HAS STAYED WITH ME. THE EIGHTH-CENTURY KOBO DAISHI IS THE MOST RENOWNED OF ALL JAPANESE SAINTS ACCORDING TO LAWRENCE BINYON, AND HE WAS NOT ONLY A PRIEST BUT A PAINTER, SCULPTOR, AND CALLIGRAPHER AS WELL. HE IS MENTIONED IN SARTON'S *Introduction*, VOL. I, P. 553.]

It will have become clear, I trust, by now that the qualities that made George Sarton the historian he was made him also something else, and gave him the intangible personal quality which elicits a letter such as I received the other day from my unknown correspondent. My father's first ambition had been to become a poet and a novelist—as a young man he even published works of fiction under an assumed name. *Isis* provided this buried poet and humanist with a platform. Over the forty years of his editorship my father wrote a great many short prefaces—they were known among his intimates as "Sarton's little sermons," and there were people who subscribed to *Isis* (not historians of science, these) for the pleasure of reading them. On the other hand, it must be confessed that they irritated some professional scholars, among them L. J. Henderson, who scolded him bitterly for these "sentimental self-indulgences." They are to a large extent statements of faith, battle cries if you will. When George Sarton wrote a biographical portrait such as that in "Communion with Erasmus," the degree of his identification with

the subject was intense; when he talked of the slow begin-
ner, the Ugly Duckling, he was really speaking from his own
inwardness.

The fact is that he consistently reached out, not only toward scholars in the field, but toward all men and women
of good will. And I have come to understand since his death,
whatever the "professionals" may sometimes wish to deny,
that just because of this tendency toward self-dramatization
he reached a much wider public than scholars usually do, or
even wish to do.

How beautiful that he was allowed to die as he wished,
in harness, on his way to deliver a lecture in Montreal, he
who had written shortly before, "To die suddenly is like
taking the wrong bus, and that bus flies out of the road to
the stars . . . in spite of all my recriminations, I am still at
heart a Platonist. . . ."

He could die with a sense of accomplishment rare in human life. The notation in the journal for Sunday 4809.03
might as well refer to himself: "It is clear to me that the main
purpose of a man's life is to give others what is in him. Such
a matter is not a question of selfishness or unselfishness. Mozart was probably rather selfish in a childish way, but he
gave the world what was in him (he could not help it) and
what a gift!

"We only have what we are, and we only have what we
give. That is, we only have what we are, but on condition
that we give all that is in us."

Mabel Elwes Sarton

TWO

Mabel Elwes Sarton

Portrait of the Artist
as My Mother

EARLY THIS MORNING when I went out to spray the roses, I found them clustered over by Japanese beetles, and it brought back a vivid memory of my mother with a bowl of soapy water in one hand, brushing them off with fury; so I went in to get a bowl of soapy water myself. Perhaps because at last I have a garden of my own I can begin to write of my mother now so long after her death in November of 1950, for until now it had seemed impossible. Every day I find myself doing things that I learned from watching her in her garden in Cambridge—the longed-for garden that came into her life in the last twenty years, the garden where she and my father spent so many peaceful hours together when he came back from Widener and she lay on a chaise longue with the tea tray beside her. Often they sat there until the light faded, savoring this pause in the arduous day. It was the only time when I think of them as resting, those two, each as high-strung as a racehorse.

My mother was an early morning person, a lark rather than an owl. She was often awake by four, plagued by recurrent migraine. Then she stole down to the kitchen to make a saving cup of tea and, safely back in bed, the tea on a tray and Cloudy, the silvery cat, lying beside her, sometimes was able to write a letter, or read for an hour. The book at hand might well be one on Chinese pottery, or a bound copy of *The Connoisseur*. For late in her life, when she could no longer earn in other ways, she pitted her knowledge of English china and Chinese pottery against the experts, came back from auctions with marvelous "finds" that she resold later on. She spent hours in the Museum of Fine Arts learning more and more useful lore for this "game" which was a delight, but also had a serious purpose. For my mother was haunted by the needs of a series of real and adopted relatives, and in this way she could send off a little help to her brother in Mexico, or the old Russian princess in Florence. Once in a while the game came out brilliantly, as when she picked up a curious object in an antique shop for $2.50, did some sleuthing in the museum, and decided it might be a Gothic horn. It was, and sold at Christie's for two hundred and fifty pounds!

Sometimes seed catalogues were the avenue to an early morning excursion. What if she had ten dollars to spend? Would it be for English asters? Lilies? Iris? Imaginary gardens flowered in her head.

By six she and Cloudy were ready to go out to taste the morning and do some work in the real garden. So by the time most of the world was just waking up, she had already lived the most intense and rewarding hours of her day. People thought of my mother as frail—and in fact she rarely felt well—but when I think of what she asked of herself in an average day when she was past seventy, I see her as a fountain of energy, flowing up in a sparkling plume, then dying down gradually toward three o'clock when she had a short rest, only to spring to life when my father came home at teatime, and rousing itself to a last display when, after listening to music for an hour with him in his study, she went down to cook the evening meal.

"Petit Coq" had been my father's nickname for her before they were married, and there was indeed a fierce little cock inside her who never died, élan vital, the spur that got her through every ordeal, and would not be denied.

How can I capture her essence? What was it, for instance, that made us laugh so much that tears poured down our cheeks, in the sheer gaiety of a moment that has vanished? Laughter is the one thing memory cannot recapture—it is gone, gone like the garden that became a jungle two years after her death.

But there are things words may hope to capture before it is too late. I think, for instance, of my mother's quick light feet, walking as fast as some people run, on the innumerable errands Petit Coq commanded. At Thanksgiving and at Easter she always took flowers to special friends. There could be no question of ordering from a florist—far too expensive! She took the streetcar into Boston to the wholesale flower market, bought several bunches which she carried home to divide and arrange, and then set out again to deliver them herself on foot. At the end of that day Petit Coq may have felt rather exhausted, but I have an idea that he gave a faint triumphant crow, "I did it! I did what I wanted to do!"

My father took the stance that he had "a frail wife" as one way of getting out of social engagements, an innocent enough white lie, except that it ended by creating a legend that almost obscured the reality—*what* this "frail wife" actually accomplished. Frail? Well, perhaps, as the Venetian

glass was frail that survived the war in our house in Wondelgem when heavy chairs did not survive.

If George Sarton was extraordinary in his uncompromising determination to do what he had it in him to do, Mabel
Sarton was extraordinary in her protean capacity to compromise many times with her own gifts for the sake of his work.
To this her life had been committed from the beginning of
their relationship, for he had warned her, "I shall always put
my work before you or any child we may have." She believed
in the vision that drove him; they worked for it together all
the days of their lives. Nevertheless she was a person in her
own right, a person with more to give to life than her genius
for recreating a home wherever we were—and how many
times was she transplanted? Even in Cambridge we had four
different apartments or houses.

She was, first of all, and would always remain, an artist, if
to be an artist is to feel the need to find expression for life
in some form outside the self. Mabel Elwes at one time or another painted miniatures and designed furniture professionally; she designed embroidered dresses, also professionally;
she taught applied design; and late in her life designed
textiles and wrote short stories. Being an artist is a matter
of essence. And success is very often a matter of luck! In her
life as an artist, the odds were against Mabel Elwes Sarton.
They might not have remained so against Mabel Elwes, but
when Sarton was added to her name, she took on partial
responsibility for someone else's creation. Petit Coq was
often frustrated, and it is proof of her (or his!) valiance and
gaiety that it has only become plain to me now how many
times the will to do something of her own had to be reborn,
and in how many guises.

Eleanor Mabel Elwes was born near London, the daughter of Gervase Elwes, of the old Suffolk family, and of
Eleanor Cole. Elwes was a civil engineer and spent years in

India, where he designed the bridges for one of the first railroads in the Himalayas, and worked also in Spain, and in Canada, while his two children, Mabel and Hugh, were literally farmed out. Hugh, of course, was sent to boarding school, but a Victorian girl had no such opportunity, and Mabel was boarded with various families who were supposed to see to her education. For years Hugh was her only family; and she saw him only on the holidays, but those holidays were memorable. One summer in Wales when my mother was six or seven, they cut themselves a secret hiding place in a hazel hedge; another summer they had a donkey and cart and were allowed to go off together for whole days with a picnic basket beside them, and a supply of carrots and sugar, for the donkey was balky. But during the long months when Mabel was left alone among strangers, she learned to depend on her own resources, to love nature passionately, and to observe it with the discriminating eyes of the solitary.

My grandmother was a vain, fiery little woman who adored her husband at the expense of her children, and between them visibly preferred her son. Fortunately Gervase Elwes was a charming and understanding father, but I wonder whether he ever realized how greatly his children, and especially Mabel, had been deprived by those long absences. There was one terrible year when she was boarded in the family of a Church of England parson. The religious household felt it their duty to bring the thirteen-year-old girl into the fold; severe pressure was put upon her to take her first communion, but they had reckoned without Mabel's fierce honesty, and without her love of her father. Gervase Elwes was one of the early Fabians, a friend of the Webbs —religious affiliation would have seemed a betrayal of his beliefs. Mabel held out, although the strain finally made her ill. Was it then, under that nearly intolerable pressure, that the migraine headaches began? My mother reacted violently at any attempt to *force* a living being, animal or human, and I see now from where that instinctive reaction sprang.

Perhaps when he came home that time her father decided that she must be given a less haphazard education; at any rate she was sent in her teens to be a student at the Institut Kherkov in Ghent. I wish I had known my grandfather. Céline Dangotte, a fellow student in Ghent, who spent a summer with the Elweses to learn English, always spoke of him with the greatest love and admiration. He was her ideal of an English gentleman with his full beard, blue eyes sparkling behind glasses, infinite courtesy, delightful humor. Céline never failed to speak of the tender inflection of his "Nellie dear," and his quizzical indulgent look at his wife across the table. His letters show an abiding curiosity about and ability to understand people of other cultures—a trait inherited by his son, who became a mining engineer in Mexico.

When Mabel was nineteen, and an art student in London, her father died suddenly of a heart attack, leaving the family not only bereft, but nearly penniless. He had lost his capital in a venture in Rhodesian mines, and had not told "Nellie dear" what the situation was, for he had expected, of course, to recoup eventually. Mabel learned the news of his death in the most brutal possible way when she came home from school. Her Uncle Edward, the solicitor, met her at the door and without a word to soften the blow blurted out "Your father's dead. Where are the keys?" He then commanded her to go out into the garden, herself, and tell her mother what had happened. The shock was terrible, worse because there was no security to fall back on, and she and her mother had never been on intimate terms.

What to do? How to live? Perhaps the head of the Institut in Belgium heard of her plight; at any rate she finally went back there, no longer as a paying boarder, but in the anomalous position of a kind of governess who took the students on walks, helped them with their English, and was paid next to nothing. It was humiliating, the more so since the rich snobbish students rubbed the humiliation in. Céline Dangotte, a few years younger, who had looked up to Mabel Elwes as an adored older girl before the calamity, now became her defender, and introduced her to her own family. Madame Dangotte rescued Mabel from the school and set her to work designing for her interior decorating firm, La Maison Dangotte; she took her into the house and treated her as her own daughter.

Who could have foreseen that the return to Ghent under such a shadow would end in transplanting happily to another language, another culture, and eventually marriage, and that Mabel Elwes would give her English heart to Belgium?*

The shock of her father's death had been cruel, but the worst shock, a shock from which she never recovered, was to come ten years later. When Mabel Elwes was engaged to be married, and sent to England for her birth certificate, she learned *then*, with no preparation at all, that she had been born before her parents' marriage and was legally illegitimate. The story is not shameful. Before he met Eleanor Cole, Gervase Elwes had been half engaged to a young woman who became fatally ill with tuberculosis. Rather than destroy the illusions of a dying girl, Nellie and Gervase waited until after her death to marry, and during that time lived as man and wife, and bore one child, Mabel. The whole affair was understood in the family, since Edward Elwes and his wife even traveled in Switzerland with the lovers. For that romantic pair, it all came right in the end. But for my mother, penniless and in poor health, to learn about it as she

* See "The Fervent Years, in *I Knew a Phoenix*.

did, thirty years later, when the fact was certain to shame
her in the eyes of her fiancé's bourgeois family, was hard indeed. Grief, even acute grief, brings its own catharsis with
it; humiliation does not. Humiliation caused by the one person in whom a young woman has put perfect trust can last
a lifetime.

I have decided to speak of this because it has explained
to me certain mysterious facets of my mother's character.
She never, for instance, had anything to do with the Elwes
side of the family; on the whole she disliked meeting English
people; it was only by accident that I found out what a distinguished name she bore, and that was after her death.

If her response seems exaggerated, as it undoubtedly
was, to what had not been after all a dishonorable situation,
we have to remember that Mabel Elwes was marrying outside her own culture into a conventional family who were
not enthusiastic about the choice George Sarton had made.
In their view a penniless English artist, in frail health, seven
years older than he, could hardly be called a good match!
Later they came to love her, but that did not help at the
time, when she had to pay a formal call on each of George's
formidable uncles to explain matters. Fortunately one of
these painful calls was on my father's aunt, Mère Marie
d'Agréda, Superior in the order of Marie-Réparatrice. My
mother never forgot her plain wise face, her compassionate
understanding, or her beautiful blue habit.

Luckily Mabel found staunch support in her own friends,
two women as different as night from day. Madeleine Van
Thorenburg, the daughter of rich wine merchants, was a
sculptor of considerable reputation. Gentle and mysterious as
a small exquisite moth, she lived her life all in inwardness, in
her studio, and behind the heavy velvet curtains of the family
mansion. She had a delicious sense of humor and knew how
to tease without wounding; she teased Mabel by calling her

"ma petite perfection." I saw her several times after my mother's death and it was she who told me how she heard the awful sobbing that lasted a whole night in the room next to hers when my mother learned the hard facts of her birth.

It was natural to have confided in Madeleine, for Madeleine had been instrumental in bringing Mabel and George together after a long year of separation. I have never known what the conflict was, nor am I quite certain about the sequence of events. I do know that before she was thirty Mabel Elwes had thought that miniature painting would be her career, and she was beginning to get commissions as well as prizes at art shows. I have here in my house a stunning sketch for a miniature of Wagner's niece, for instance. But Mabel had a nervous breakdown, and after it her hand shook so badly that further work in that art was out of the question. So she was trying to mend both a broken heart and a broken career when she went to Zurich to study bookbinding.

Madeleine was quick to see, on Mabel's return, that her heart, at least, had not mended, and she persuaded her to attempt a reconciliation. "George loves you, but he will never make the first move. You will have to go to him." So she did, that very day. Rather typically, for he was always romantic about the religious life, George had rented a cell in an old monastery, and was working there. The parted lovers became engaged that very afternoon and celebrated by a long row in a boat along the Lys. It was the first day of spring, 1910.

The other supportive friend was, of course, Céline Dangotte. In Céline my mother had found an idealist as anxious to give to life, as unconventional as she herself was; but Céline and her fiancé, Raymond Limbosch, the poet, were equally doubtful about Mabel and George's marriage. I have in my possession a long passionate letter from him, outlining with real insight exactly what a marriage to George Sarton would mean, how little understanding he had of human

relations, how emotionally immature the eccentric young man
who suffered all his life from the lack of a mother's care when
he was an infant would prove to be as a life companion. He
was right, of course. But reason could not alter true love, and
true love was there, on both sides.

It had been a long struggle, but Mabel looked back on
those years before her marriage as rich ones. The city of
Ghent, so beautiful in itself, was a ferment of artistic and
political life. My mother, brought up as a Fabian, felt at
home among the Socialist students in Belgium; she was involved in their attempt to cross the bridge between the intellectuals and young working men and women, and was one
of the moving spirits in an informal group who called themselves the *Flinken*. This was a mixed group of working girls
and students who met periodically to listen to lectures and
to engage in passionate discussions about art and life in
general: feminists (the men called the women by their last
names), socialists, pacifists, vegetarians, they read Morris,
Ruskin, Ibsen, Maeterlinck, Shaw, Verhaeren; they went on
long walks; they wrote each other letters, so the discussion
could be carried on between meetings. By the time Mabel
Elwes was thirty, she had not only been considerably buf-
feted by fate; she had grown into a human being of strong
convictions and of real power.

How peaceful, then, the house in Wondelgem must have
seemed, where she and George settled into their married life.
At last she would have a home of her own, a garden, a chance
to put down roots, a chance to breathe. It was all created in
a fervor of happiness. She designed much of the furniture
herself, for she was now working for Céline Dangotte Limbosch, who after her marriage moved her mother's business
to Brussels, and the furniture was made at the Arts Décoratifs—ADCD—there. She and George hunted out old chests
in antique shops (Ghent teems with them), a huge desk filled

with pigeonholes and secret drawers for her, a long refectory table for him to work at; they had curtains made of fine Belgian linen; bookcases were built. And while Mabel worked in the garden, George worked away sending out announcements of the first issue of *Isis*, the International Quarterly on the history of science that he edited for more than forty years. On Sundays the old friends came out from Ghent; Mabel could invite her mother over from England for visits now and then, and George could invite his uncles, who were soon won over to the marriage . . . for who could resist the charm of all this?

"Wondelgem" . . . the word is full of radiance for me, because of the tone in my mother's voice whenever she spoke its name. I myself do not remember it, nor my nurse, or the big black dog who had to be given away because he was so jealous of me, nor my infant brother who died a few hours after he was born. All I know is that my parents had four marvelous years there before the world upheaval of 1914 sent us, as it did so many others, out into exile.

We found our way eventually to the United States to begin again from scratch. For George Sarton this transplanting proved to be beneficent: he found support for his work in the Carnegie Institution and no such help would have been forthcoming in Belgium. But for my mother it was a second transplanting, and she was now over thirty. She had been on the brink of making a name for herself as a designer of modern furniture; a suite was to have been shown in August 1914 in Brussels, at an international exhibition. She would certainly have gone on doing distinguished work for the ADCD, Céline's firm. As I write I look at one of the pieces rescued from a cellar after the war and bought by my father as a surprise. The Japanese influence, the simplicity of line, and the charming brilliant inlaid wreaths of flowers make this desk a magnificent example of Art Nouveau. As a

matter of fact, whenever we went back to Belgium she did
some designing, and in 1924 won a gold medal at the international exhibition of decorative arts in Paris for an embroidered altarpiece. Mabel Sarton was no amateur who dabbled
in the arts, but a serious professional, recognized as such.

But although she met the second transplanting to America with amazing resilience, she never again found such a
life-giving group of intimates as those she had left in Belgium. Never again would she feel herself so much a maker
in a world a-making—and for more than twenty years there
would not be another garden.

But in 1916 she did not look back; she began at once to try
to find ways to help my father financially. While we lived in
Washington, D.C., she found a partner interested in launch-
ing a firm to design and build simple inexpensive modern
furniture. But the partner, a charming woman, was black, and
Mabel Sarton was soon informed that that could not work in
the land of the free and the home of the brave. It was a harsh
introduction to American culture.

Not until we settled at last in Cambridge, Massachusetts,
in 1918 did she begin to feel at home. There we lived in a
tiny three-room apartment, and there we found the Shady
Hill School. It was lifesaving. Not only was I given the best
education possible, but the school gave my mother a chance
to become part of a working group whose aspirations she
could share. Founded by Agnes and Ernest Hocking and run
by them, the school was a cooperative, and the parents
themselves did much of the teaching. My mother invented
her own subject, applied design, and her own inventive ways
of teaching it. I can still see the rows of round ice cream
boxes which we transformed into delightful objets d'art by
covering them with geometric designs in brilliant colors, for
she had a genius for bringing a child to understand the
pleasure of playing with simple forms, and a daring and

distinguished sense of color. Her classrooms became Aladdin's caves, where splendor emerged from the simplest materials.

For years Mabel Sarton not only taught applied design at Shady Hill and, later on, at the Winsor School in Boston, but she was the designer for a firm in Washington, D.C., a firm she and Margaret Gillespie, the business manager, founded together. Belgart, as it was called, created dresses, summer dresses, evening dresses, woolen, silk, cotton, all embroidered with brilliant designs of birds and flowers. They were influenced by folk art, folk art used with a unique imagination and inventiveness. My mother went to Washington twice a year to make the designs for the embroidery (someone else did the work of couturier) and to teach the group of women who executed it in bold combinations of wool and silk, familiar to us now in the fashionable crewelwork. The results were soon picked up, not only by individual buyers such as Nazimova but also by the great stores, Lord & Taylor, Marshall Field, and Neiman Marcus.

When she went off to Washington for ten days at a time, she could be exclusively her artist self. I feel her exhilaration when, every so often, someone I do not know sends me a dress, folded and kept for forty years because it seemed such a treasure. In the end the business failed from sheer success: they could not finance what had become sizable demands in the wholesale market. But for years Mabel Sarton was able to put almost as much as her husband into the till. She paid my school expenses, sent me to camp, bought my clothes out of what she had earned. And by doing that she made it possible for George Sarton to go on publishing *Isis*, mostly at his own expense. But, feminist though he was theoretically, my father did not like his wife to work, and never acknowledged to her or to others that for many years it had been a partnership financially. Was it the Belgian bourgeois in him who objected so strongly and who could not be generous about what she had accomplished? I do not know. I only know that he refused absolutely to go over accounts, and since he was unrealistic about what life costs, even for a small family such as ours, never gave my mother enough for household expenses. In this marriage, so good and fruitful in every other way, money remained a cruel thorn. But at least for those years of Belgart Mabel Sarton, or Petit Coq, was able to fill in the gap, and to do it in a joyful way.

When my mother was over forty she became pregnant. The Limbosches never forgave my father for allowing this to happen since he had been warned that the birth would be a risky business for his wife. Nevertheless, when the time came for her to go to the hospital, he contrived to be in New York! I find this almost unbelievable, but his letters from a New York club welcoming little Alfred into the world prove it to be true. Did he even see that red-faced little boy who died in the hospital after five days? I did and I remember him well, in a white ruffled cap. And I remember the atmosphere of grief. The bassinet so lovingly prepared, the new shelves where baby clothes had been folded ready to welcome him, were taken away. There was a terrible darkness and emptiness in the bedroom, and my mother did not come home for a month. She went to stay with friends. It is clear to me now that she was fighting serious depression. It was no doubt a time of agonizing reappraisal for her—of her marriage, of her life itself. And the whole episode retained a nightmare quality in her mind. More than once she described how she and my father went to Annisquam with the ashes, hoping to bury them in the ocean they both loved. Instead, it turned out to be low tide; crabs scuttled about in the black ooze. That image stayed with her. It had been traumatic.

All this rich living and dying in a hundred ways is in the face I have before me as I write, in a photograph dated 1924 when Mabel Elwes Sarton was forty-three. Already the hair around the open brow is white, although the long bands she wound around her head made a casque of chestnut brown. We do not get the full impact of those luminous gray eyes because she is looking down, reflective and aloof. But the beauty of the eyelids is there, the pure mold in which those eyes were set, the straight English nose, the firm, sensitive mouth. I had not noticed until now what a strong chin completes the oval.

However true to an essence it may be, a portrait of this kind freezes a single mood. This is my mother's face as though captured in solitude. I recognize it only in part, because it is too static. Moods flowed through that beautiful casing as variable as New England weather. She was sudden and merry; tears came quickly to her eyes, tears of laughter, tears of anger or grief; she could blaze up like a tree on fire with indignation before oppression anywhere; she could be mischievous and airy; but whatever she did, she did with the utmost intensity, even simply looking at a flower. So too she looked at paintings, or a piece of Chinese pottery, or an animal. She read enormously, could be highly critical, and when she was convinced, could be convincing, as when she writes to her husband, "I have finished Maritain; it is a grave and beautiful book, and you must read it —it looks so deep, so far, so quietly. It is free of passion, but full of feeling, and of faith. You must read it as soon as possible."

I have hardly ever been in my parents' presence without listening to a discussion about a book one of them had discovered—Isak Dinesen, Freya Stark, these were events in the household. There was between my parents a constant exchange about all the things that mattered most to them—

books, gardens, music, art, politics—and their differences of
temperament made these exchanges rich. Their ways of attacking a museum or an exhibition were characteristic. My
father, omnivorous and indefatigable, looked at every single
object and made copious notes. My mother did not attempt
to see everything, but spent a long time absorbing a single
painting, a Cézanne, a Turner, a Vermeer, or a piece of ancient pottery. At the end of two hours they met again to
exchange and discuss what each had found memorable.

How much my mother taught me about respect for
animals, for she understood their need for privacy and
dignity! Any cruelty distressed her and in its presence she
acted at once—even to the point of pursuing Cloudy into
the cellar and extracting a mouse from her jaws to set it
free! I can see her work-worn hands, gardener's hands, holding a Worcester or Chelsea cup and turning it slowly, her
head slightly bent to one side, in just the way she might look
at the cat, appreciating each thing for its own quality and,
above all, paying attention as few people do.

Children were drawn to her, especially little boys
(shades of those two dead infants of her own). At Channing
Place Binks Barett, then about six, used to come to watch
her garden, and soon she was teaching him how to help.
How touched she was when he gave her a small gardening
cart that Christmas! Once he asked her whether I was *her*
mother, a delightful instance of the sense of equality she
had created although her face was wrinkled then, and she
was in her sixties.

Nothing my mother touched, a bunch of flowers, a table
setting, the arrangement of a room, a person in doubt about
his value—there was nothing that did not bear the mark
of her genius to fashion it closer to some magic within it
which her eye and her heart sensed, and which she longed
to make clear. "She taught me so much," I hear from all her

friends. It was an unconscious teaching, for she never said a
didactic word or imposed herself. She called out the essence
of others because she was so vividly able to communicate
her own.

She could not stand any sort of sanctimoniousness or
pretentiousness. She had an unerring eye for the false. But
she could always meet deep feeling on its own level, without sentimentality, with a kind of honesty and compassion
that had healing in them. From her I learned that whatever
one gives, the gift may turn bitter if one withholds oneself.
She had to be involved in any life she touched. For instance,
no check was ever sent to the old Russian princess in Florence, whom she helped support for many years, without a
long personal letter, nor did she hide her own anxieties and
problems. She could not conceive of friendship on a superficial level nor be anything but irritated by mundane conversation. So she found social occasions exhausting and in
the end solitude rather than personal relationships became
the well from which she drew her strength.

In the last twenty years she had need of strength. How
hard she had worked all her life! But she had never had to
do the general housework and cooking; the other day I
came upon a letter to my father in which she discusses ways
of cutting down on expenses; she had to write because it
was impossible to discuss such matters with him. In the letter she says she will give up anything, even the dear house
at Channing Place and the garden, *except* "the services of
a maid." Yet the time came when she had to give that up because a general maid, living in, had become horrendously
expensive. My mother was an excellent cook and seemed to
have inexhaustible energy, but during those years she was
ill. Not only illness but two serious operations had to be
met. However, it was not the physical strain that really mattered. Petit Coq still had the élan vital to master that. It

was that she felt immolated, expecially when my father, on
his physician's advice, decided to work only half days at
Widener, and so came home for a late lunch. What she had
lost was her freedom to go off to the museum for the day,
and the long hours when she could slowly recover from
migraine, and not hurry. The housework broke rather
brutally into this pattern. She felt caught, more caught
than she had felt during all the years of poverty and struggle before. And, as far as I know, my father never once took
her out to dinner; so she was a full-time maid without even
a day off. Yet there were compensations, one very real. My
parents would not have shared those long hours listening
to recorded music in his study after tea if the cook had been
waiting impatiently to serve dinner—they sometimes did
not go down till after eight. Here there was communion
and rest for her, and for him.

My mother was not a saint, thank heaven, and only a saint
could have endured without protest my father's impervious
lack of understanding, especially about money. During
those last years she suffered from terrible blighting rages
which she fought out alone, sometimes not emerging back
into clear air for weeks at a time. Could the wound in their
marriage have been healed if she had fought it out at the
very beginning in Wondelgem? For it all began there—my
father's anger about what she spent, and at the same time
his refusal to go over accounts with her or face the facts
of what life cost. By the time she was seventy it was surely
too late—and by then she had formed the habit of control,
of never letting him guess what she was suffering, because
she so honored his work and knew only too well how driven
he was by it.

Driven herself by the need to make money somehow to
be able to go on helping the Russians, as well as her brother,
Hugh, in Mexico, she tried in those last years in three new

ways to use her talents. For one whole year she worked on textile designs, but failed to market them—she was not a businesswoman, and where, anyway, could she have found time and energy to make the rounds of the manufacturers? She also experimented with painted designs on organdy for evening dresses—those brilliant bunches of flowers came back in a new guise—but, lovely as they were, she never succeeded in finding an outlet for them. Finally she spent many early morning hours in bed writing short stories, but they were not quite good enough to be accepted by the magazines. What is amazing to me is what fecundity of spirit she had! She never stopped creating, even when life at the end used her as a cart horse instead of the racehorse she was. She went on creating, willy-nilly, because she had to, because she needed those moments of pure delight when the imagination flowers alone in order to survive—because she was an artist.

I shall not dwell on her last illness, except to evoke three images which are relevant to the essential person. After a summer when we had faced together, all three, that my mother had a limited time to live—the mastectomy had been performed too late and the cancer spread to the lungs—and had faced too that I could not continue as full-time nurse and housekeeper, as I was committed to a first year of teaching freshman English at Harvard, we began to look for a housekeeper. I interviewed many prospects, but either they themselves seemed too old and frail, or were scared off by the tragic circumstances. Often mother felt too ill to see them herself. But, fortunately, on the day I found myself talking with a middle-aged Irish woman with a lovely tranquil face and clear blue eyes, my mother did ask Julia Martin to come up for a few minutes. After that interview Julia agreed to help us out. She told me later that her family had tried to dissuade her. "What do you want to go to that sick woman for?

She'll wear you out!" Julia answered, "I like her face." So
that beautiful face once more exerted its spell, one last time,
old and wrinkled though it was. And what a blessing Julia
became, for she was a splendid cook, a natural nurse, a faithful friend, and I often heard her laughing with my mother,
up to the end.

The second image of those last months is that of my
father's tender care, a startling image because she had mothered him through all their years together, and he had never
been able to make those little gestures of love most husbands
do find ways of making. Now that Mabel was dying he got
up at five (hardly able to open his eyes) when she rang a
little bell, went down, and made her a saving cup of tea. He
had, until then, never learned even how to boil water! My
guilt about having left the house in the last weeks (we had
imagined it might be two years) flows away, for had I been
there, my mother would not have been cherished in just this
way by her husband. How good that he was able to mother
her a little, after all!

The third scene I wish to evoke took place close to the
end. A box of old china had arrived from England, but my
mother had felt too weak to open it, until suddenly one afternoon she demanded that the box be brought up, and we
opened it for her. For a half hour we saw again the delight,
the mischief, as her wan face turned pink with excitement,
and she cried out, as she pulled forth an English Lowestoft
cup and saucer, "I *must* get down once more to put this in
the collection!" There it was—the fountain springing to life;
Petit Coq had come back to bid us a last farewell. And although she never did get downstairs, I carry this image in
my heart like an emblem of the whole life—hungry, elated,
life-enhancing, discriminating, passionate.

Part II

—Claire Limbosch

Céline Dangotte Limbosch

THREE

Céline Dangotte Limbosch

SHE WAS THERE at the very beginning, in fact held me in her
arms an instant after I was born, before my mother did. She
is the only person I have ever known who remembered Gervase Elwes, my English grandfather. She loved my mother
passionately when they were at school together in Ghent,
and never ceased to do so through the whole of her long
life. And she always called me her eldest child.

So Céline Dangotte Limbosch has been an integral part
of my life, and when she died the other day, at ninety-three,
I felt as though my childhood had fallen like a cliff into the
sea. Who remembers my mother as a young woman now?
Who remembers me as an infant?

My first European memories are of the Pignon Rouge,

the Limbosch's house and garden near Brussels. After we
had lived in city apartments in Washington, D.C., and then
Cambridge, Massachusetts, for the first four years of our
exile, what bliss it was to be able to run wild in a huge
garden where I could get lost among the rhododendrons at
the back or walk sedately all the way round the formal borders of flowers, and across a small orchard, or sit secretly in
the arbor, a round house made of leaves where a small child
was invisible from the outside, or venture into the immaculate rows of the *potager* and steal a pea pod to suck, or search
for duck and goose eggs under the flowering bushes.

In America I had been allowed no pet, for my father
worked at home those first years, and even the goldfish we
tried disturbed him with their *pp . . .pp* when they came up
for air! What bliss then to find myself in a peaceable kingdom
of kittens, cats, dogs, ducks, geese, hens, and a goat, to be
a wild child in a safe wilderness, bounded and protected by
love, and, above all, to find myself part of a family! For
every only child is nostalgic about family life and especially
one as often uprooted as I had been. Perhaps what I had
needed most when we first went back in 1919 and I was
seven, was Céline herself, "Mamie," as I called her, her
earthiness, her physical warmth. I basked in the moral world
she inhabited where values were certainly oversimplified, a
restful black-and-white world, both dramatic and orderly.

She and Papa (her husband, Raymond) were away all
day at the Arts Décoratifs, her business in Brussels. We
waved them off at the gate and then ran back to be taken
over by BoBo, the German governess who gave us lessons
and taught us to sew, with whom we went for walks in the
forest, and who was all that a good nanny can be, a humorous always just disciplinarian with a gaunt ageless face, blue
eyes, and frizzy hair, who scolded us with a rough voice full
of tenderness and a twinkle in her eye. But the real excite-

ment of the day was the return of Mamie and Papa in the
evening. We rushed out, everyone screaming with joy, to be
hugged, and then to be commandeered like a small willing
army, to help Mamie in the garden. I can hear her voice
shouting, *"Allons, les enfants, dépêchez vous!"* One of our
evening chores was to line up like a fire brigade and pass
buckets of water along to her as she watered the vegetables.
Then after supper what bliss to climb into her big bed, the
two eldest, Claire and Jacques, and I, and, dreamy as evening
birds in this delightful nest, listen while Mamie read aloud
. . . Nils Holgerrsen was *the* book that year.

The world Céline created for me at the Pignon Rouge
and made so vivid when I was a small child remained the
only absolute continuity in my life. While we moved from
one apartment to another in Cambridge, I knew that the
Pignon Rouge and the garden would be unchanged when
we were able to go back again, as we did about every seven
years. As I grew up, it was wonderful to know that there
was one place in the world that would not change, a place
where I had been, once and for all, taken in and accepted.

There it always was, the round table under the apple tree
in the little orchard, and Mamie sitting on a bench behind it
in one of the white sunbonnets she wore, feeding crumbs
to the ducks and geese, calling each by name, as she waited
for the maid to bring out the tablecloth and cups and saucers,
bread and butter and homemade jam for tea. Afterward we
walked, arm in arm, up and down the scraped paths that
crisscrossed the lawn and garden plots, my hand clasped
firmly in hers, for a heart-to-heart talk. I remember one
vividly although it took place forty years ago, because what
she said astonished me and still does. At that time I was in
love with a man twice my age and married; we were lovers.
Céline grew thoughtful as I told her about it, about my
doubts and anxieties, and suddenly she turned to me quite

gravely and said, "I don't think you'll ever marry, and perhaps you should not. You will always have love affairs."

It was astonishing that she set her seal in that way on my
life, for in relation to her own children, at least in one similar
circumstance, she was harsh, puritanical, and unforgiving for
years. It was less surprising that she understood so well my
passionate attachments to women, for she herself had certainly loved my mother violently and possessively when they
were young, and perhaps her indulgence in regard to me
sprang from that deep root. Whenever we met she never
failed to talk about my mother, whom she repeatedly told
me had been the greatest moral influence in her life. As
Céline grew older, into her eighties, and as I grew into middle age I sometimes found that my mother as exemplar had
ceased to have any reality and had become a kind of whitewashed myth. It didn't matter, for by then I had accepted
Céline as a total human being, flawed as we all are, as she
had accepted me long before.

What was she really like? I had asked myself the question many times long before she died. "Who was he?" a re-
cently widowed friend asked me about her husband at the
end of a letter. Who are they, those we have loved and suffered from, and judged and lived beside, and whose essential
being has remained mysterious because we find it hard to
make an understandable whole out of such disparate characteristics or to separate the essence from the effects upon
ourselves of such paradoxical components?

When she welcomed a guest, her bare feet in sandals, her
glasses slipping down her nose, her strong hands those of a
gardener, her sunbonnet with its Kate Greenaway look, who
could have guessed (she herself never did) that Céline was
playing a role? At school she had acted a bit, and even
played *l'Aiglon* . . . she recited poetry in a rather Comédie
Française theatrical way . . . and now she was playing the

role of the lady who has chosen to be a countrywoman for purely romantic reasons. When Colette made her speech of acceptance at the Royal Academy of Letters in Brussels, she too chose to appear in bare feet in sandals and to emphasize in every possible way, while she praised the Comtesse de Noailles, that she herself was a crude peasant. Everyone except Céline, who was delighted no doubt because she recognized herself without knowing in what way there was a similarity, saw through Colette's chosen mask.

Actors need in their audience adorers who do not see through the mask, who will believe what they have chosen to pretend they are. And it was this that explained, perhaps, why Céline always longed for new friends, reached out endearingly and with such fresh response to any new arrival into her circle; for then—at least for a time—she could play her role before an innocent audience. The trouble was that very soon these newfound friends began to feel troubled. The delight of instant intimacy, the confidences exchanged, the strong warm hand held out, began to seem in some strange way a danger, and before they knew what was happening, Céline had taken them over, was persuading them into decisions they were not ready to make, was (or so it might seem) attacking their authentic being and forcing them to play roles they had no wish to play. So instant intimacy was too often followed by disillusion.

She showed her genius in her relation to animals, small children, and with the servant girls whom she trained, mothered, believed in, and saw happily married—girls who were on probation and under the supervision of a judge of the children's court. Here her qualities of commanding general in the war against sloth, carelessness, laissez-faire, were wholly beneficial. She knew how to praise as well as to criticize, and she could tame dragons with her mixture of charm and authoritarianism.

At first glance her marriage to Raymond Limbosch seemed a perfect balance of opposites, her warm earthiness balancing his intellectualism, her talent for business and for organizing and running things balancing his need for meditation, her supportive belief in him balancing his need for recognition. And in the early years of their marriage there is no doubt that they were deeply in love, and that love fulfilled in four beautiful children, three girls and a boy—and in Raymond's early books of poems, lyrical celebrations of their happiness. Then Céline made a mistake. A Belgian poet writing in French rather than Flemish must be published in France to make a name. Raymond had not found a publisher and was temperamentally unsuited to wooing the critics. She suffered with and for him, and finally persuaded him to let her pay for publication. Of course she thought she was giving him what he most wanted, but she was actually, if not emasculating him, turning him into an amateur, saving him from the humiliations of knocking on publishers' doors at the cost of his identity as a writer.

After they had survived two world wars, after they had lost their only son in a traffic mountaineering accident at seventeen, as they became middle-aged and then old, the opposites that had seemed to make a balance became too harsh. Céline was tremendously healthy and Raymond never well. She was puritanical and he needed small luxuries, cigarettes, elegant clothing, warmth in the house (he was always cold and became infuriated at the slightest draught), and suffered for lack of them. He spent fortunes on what she felt were unnecessary medicines, while she worked too hard to save pennies. Raymond's pent-up irritations burst out into bad tempers and, even worse, complete withdrawal to his study for days at a time.

Céline reacted by overplaying the role of humble and adoring wife, and it grated to see this happening, for she was the real power; she ruled the household and always had. Is family life always a mixture of hell and heaven? I who had basked in the heaven of it when I was a small child now became aware of the hell as I went back year after year to stay at the Pignon Rouge, loving them both and slowly growing up to become a friend rather than an adopted daughter to each.

Yet somehow the life-giving atmosphere was sustained, especially on Sundays when we were ten or twelve at table as friends from Brussels came out for a day in the country. As always we went into the salon for demitasses and long philosophical arguments after dinner. Here at least Raymond did dominate and sometimes read his newest work—so much of it never to be published—or launched into a long oral meditation for, after days in his study, he was full of ideas that needed airing.

But those years after World War II were difficult years for Céline. The business had to be sold. Servants were hard to find, and the only ones available Spanish or Italian girls. It was typical of her that she painstakingly gave them French lessons and herself tried to learn Spanish and Italian, her efforts sometimes leading to gales of laughter. Raymond had to be nursed through one psychosomatic or real illness after another. Playing the role of countrywoman—which had been a kind of game when BoBo, as well as a cook and gardener were there to take over some of the work—had become a narrowing, imprisoning reality. There as elsewhere in the world the cost of living soared and people living on inherited money were hard put to make ends meet. Céline became fanatically parsimonious and drove herself to be as self-supporting as possible by heroic efforts in the garden, jam-making, putting up the vegetables she had sown, watered, fertilized, weeded herself alone. Only very rarely could she afford a man to do a few hours of hard digging.

The tragedy was that all those joys—and they had been real joys—had now become a frightful struggle. And when most of what one does is done for duty's sake, bitterness wells up. How did she keep herself alive? I think perhaps by her passions, for she was never really a wise person, but always a passionate one. She could still rise up after her daily reading of *Le Soir* in a rage over politics; she still read avidly, especially in the French writers of the eighteenth century, all of Sainte-Beuve, for instance, at one time. But most of all she never lost her deep feeling for nature, for animals, and her letters to me were full of descriptions of the evening light in autumn, or of the death (for instance) of Franz, the great white goose, when he was over nineteen, and how Mimisse, his only remaining mate, went into a decline as a result. What kept Céline alive into very old age was something absolutely fresh in her approach to life, as fresh as a child's, as intransigent as a child's. Where Raymond was overintellectual, she could rush in without any power of self-criticism and write short stories—one novella won a prize in a newspaper contest. She had to act her own life out as though she were a character in a play she was writing as she acted it. So up to the end all was drama and there were "big scenes" nearly every day. But, just as does a child, she suffered in exaggerated ways and poured out her anguish and dismay like a child . . . especially about the painful subject of her daughters. For they had each had to be ruthless in order to break her dominion over them, and she could never understand wholly that this had been her own doing. Nor could she understand why Raymond in the last years of his life withdrew more and more into himself, and even finally sought the help of a psychiatrist.

For me, the Pignon Rouge still remained the perfect nest for a wild bird who migrated there for a few weeks each year. I loved doing the little tasks like setting the table and washing the dishes. I loved being made again into a useful child and escaping to my room upstairs to write, as I had done for twenty years. I loved finding my mother and father so richly alive in Céline's vivid memory of them. With whom else could I talk in just this way? Walking up and down the garden paths, a little neglected now and overgrown, we went on exchanging our lives. The garden seemed as poetic as it had ever been, the purple clematis and pale pink roses as lavish over the pergola at the front door. But even while it seemed to be there, changeless forever, it was changing. Raymond died.

Then Céline was alone with Nicole, her middle daughter, who came home for the midday meal from the lycée in Brussels where she worked as a psychiatric social worker. Nicole herself was middle-aged by then and theirs an uneasy union because it had to be sustained on Céline's illusion that she was still necessary, whereas Nicole, the only child still living at home, longed to begin a life of her own. And the dear Pignon Rouge, its casement windows and heavy door always open to strangers and friends, became a prison.

Would it have been kinder of fate had Céline died there in her eighties, spading a flower bed or pruning a tree? I sometimes wondered. She was so clearly overworked and often desperate. But I never imagined that the spell could be broken as it was when the decision was made to sell the house. The three daughters installed their mother in a large beautiful apartment in Brussels. Claire came up from the South of France to supervise and use her skill as interior decorator (she had been a professional before her marriage); Nicole at last moved into a house of her own; and Jacqueline, the youngest, came often with great bunches of flowers from her own garden. The spell was broken that had kept the children prisoners and, free themselves now, they could give the withheld love for which Céline had always longed. It was really a new life.

It is a mark of her immense vitality that Céline was able to make the transition. At first her letters were poignant. In one she wrote, "I feel like a spider whose web has been broken and who does not know how to make a new one." The hardest thing was the lack of trees. Her windows looked out onto a street on one side and at the back faced other apartments over low gardens. But above the buildings she could watch the sunset, sitting in her low armchair facing the balcony. And at once she began to put out crumbs for the sparrows. She wrote me that "my room" was waiting for me, and the big desk I had always worked at had been installed in it.

Little by little she wove a new web. Relieved of cooking and gardening, she began to play a new role, no longer the countrywoman in the guise of Colette, but a lady of leisure with a servant to look after her, who could receive her friends. They too were now old, and could come to see her more often because she was near by. Mel, a very dear old friend, came every weekend when the servant was off; they picnicked together, teased each other, and argued like schoolgirls. They took little walks to the park at the end of the street. And all this I learned through Céline's nearly illegible letters (she was losing her eyesight), more frequent now that she had time.

I was soon reading longer and longer letters about Yvette, the French servant, a woman of great dignity and charm. It seemed a miracle that the children had found such a person and I was delighted to hear that Céline was taking her to the theatre and on expeditions to museums—and then I read plans to educate Yvette, to send her to art school! It was too clearly the old pattern and I dreaded the inevitable disaster, when Yvette would feel suffocated and have to break away from such a dominating passion and such illusions.

I was not able to go over to inhabit "my room" and to see Céline in this new world until after her first year there. I found her happier than I had ever known her, serene, and, most remarkable of all, all those obsessions about cooking and housework had vanished. She had been glad to abdicate and to leave everything to Yvette. It was marvelous to see Céline at last enjoying a little luxury and leisure, and basking, too, in the loving attentions of Jacqueline.

I had an attack of flu while I was there and was in bed for a few days. In the early morning and before going to bed Mamie, wearing nothing but a long vest that reached to her thighs, came into my room to see how I was. She was well over eighty, and I was astonished to see that her body, firm and delicate, was still that of a young girl! I told her so, and we laughed about it. The image has stayed with me, and gradually yielded its full significance as a metaphor. Sixty, seventy years before, she was reaching out to anyone who came under her spell with the same intensity she was now showing in relation to Yvette. For all the wars, and terribly hard work, and suffering over Raymond and her children, the amazingly youthful soul stayed as it was in an amazingly youthful body. In all the years she had not changed! And I realized that people change by coming to understand themselves, and this Céline had never been able to do. So the courage, the eagerness toward life, the love of plants and animals, the innocent passions were all there, intact, and so was the possessive, hungry, *autoritaire* only child who had never grown up.

The last years were not kind. Yvette inevitably withdrew, and there were then two helpers, night and day, neither of whom Céline liked very much. She twice fell and broke her hip, and had to be for weeks each time in a nursing home.

Then I had characteristic letters where she recounted her "taming" of various eccentric old women in the home, talking as though she herself were twenty, had no broken hip, and would soon be perfectly well. She did make astonishing comebacks, but she was now very deaf, her eyes were failing, and the last time I saw her, I was shocked to see a very old woman, suddenly grown tiny and frail. Hoping she would be able to hear my voice, I sat on a cushion at her knee, but we could not really communicate. Yet I saw the will to live life to the full still very much there as she took a copybook out that had been tucked in beside her and read me the poems she was writing . . . sometimes breaking down and laughing when she couldn't decipher her own hand. I had brought freesias, remembering how acute her sense of smell had always been, and she buried her nose in them for a moment.

If her courage failed, she did not show it. But for those close to her it seemed an interminable journey to the end. When, at last, Jacqueline's letter came to tell me she had died peacefully, and said, "It's a page turned . . . and what a page . . ." the memories flooded in, rich, happy, grateful. The enchanted world of the Pignon Rouge as I had seen it as a child was vividly with me for days, and the "Mamie" whom I adored came back once again . . .

We had learned long ago never to say good-bye, and for a good reason. When I was thirteen my mother and I spent a year at the Pignon Rouge while my father stayed in Cambridge to work. It was a difficult year for both of us. Transplanted from Shady Hill, not at home in French ways, I did badly at school and became ill. My mother was unhappy for reasons I never knew. But during that long dark winter Céline and I cemented our love and when we had to say good-bye on the train for Paris where mother and I were meeting my father after a year apart, we both cried desperately, a little theatrically perhaps, but I know I felt absolutely torn in two. And then, after that dramatic farewell, she came to join us in Paris; she had been unexpectedly named to the jury for the International Exhibition of Arts and Crafts, just about to open! We felt quite sheepish about those torrents of tears, and made a pact there and then never to say good-bye to each other.

We had a glorious time in Paris. The exhibition itself was fascinating: I remember especially a glittering reproduction of a temple from Bangkok. There was also one of the first large displays of African art from the Congo (Céline had been importing it for some time for her ADCD). My mother won a gold medal for an embroidered altarpiece that Céline had commissioned, and altogether there was an atmosphere of joyful celebration.

One day Céline took me to Versailles, and as we walked up and down the marble staircases and through the formal gardens among the fountains and orderly parterres of flowers, she peopled the whole scene for me with her vivid dramatic gift. For that afternoon we were inhabitants of the eighteenth century. It all became very real, even to the stink of excrement on the stairs, the human sweat concealed by strong perfumes and the little bouquets the women carried. We participated in the intrigues, and shared the triumph of being invited to the king's *levée* in his bedroom. For a long rich day Céline transported me in time and I was *there* at Versailles as no tourist, perhaps, has ever been.

Real theatre was in her gift to me as a child because the ADCD lent furniture and bibelots to Jules Delacre, who had a repertory company in Brussels, and in return she was always given a box. Once the play was Barrie's *Quality Street*; we children were taken to a matinée in our best white corduroy dresses that my mother had designed, each

with a different collar of bright embroidered flowers. From
our box we waved in great excitement to Jean Dominique
and Marie Gaspar, our professors at the Institut Belge de
Culture Française, and felt very important when we were
allowed to go backstage and meet the actors. That was my
first smell of theatre behind the curtain. It stayed with me,
though at that time I wanted to be a dancer.

But what my mind finally rested on after this kaleido-
scope of memories had shifted many times was Céline sitting
on the granite step of my house in Nelson, New Hampshire,
drinking a glass of milk, and suddenly silent in the beautiful autumn light after a talkative trip north from Cambridge . . . she had, in her seventies, taken a freighter alone
to come to give her blessing to my new life in the country.
My parents were dead . . . there was no one to bless this
adventure as she could do and did by making that long journey, no one who could place the dream of Nelson beside the
dream of Wondelgem, my parents' house, and encompass
them both as she did.

Of course as soon as she had caught her breath, the first
thing she did was spade up the matted, weedy front border,
and next day helped me stack a load of wood that had been
dumped in the road. And when she said, "How your mother
would have loved this house, and all you have done here!"
my cup ran over. Dear Céline, she had wanted to come when
we knew my mother was dying . . . but we felt the emotional
strain would have been too much. Were we wrong, I sometimes wonder? Perhaps not. For it was not to my mother
Mabel whom she had tried to possess, of whom she was
jealous, that Céline could give true love, but to Mabel's
child, whom she helped to grow up to strength and self-
discipline, that little May whom she could take into her
heart, and let go, on whom she never laid the slightest pres-

sure, for whom she remained to the end the dearest friend.

When I was a small child, I called her Mamie because she was truly a mother to me; later on, after I was grown up, she became Aunty Lino, and then simply Lino. In the last years she was for me, as she had been for my mother, Céline, an equal. When I was her patient, Marynia Farnham once said to me, "When one has completely had an experience, there is no grief when it ends." So it is, I believe, for Céline and me. We never said good-bye after that one time, and now we never will. The experience had been rich, deep, sustaining, and wholly beneficent.

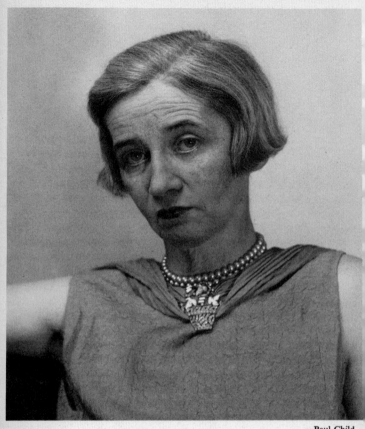

—Paul Child

Edith Forbes Kennedy

FOUR

Edith Forbes Kennedy

EDITH KENNEDY has been dead for more than thirty years, since September 18th, 1942, but her presence is as vivid to me today as though I had just run in to the little house on Shepard Street in Cambridge, Massachusetts, to listen to some Mozart and, between records, talk about art and life. Casual and open as that house was to friends of all ages who came and went at any hour of day or night—the door was never locked—there was one taboo: you listened and did not talk while music was being played. Had a person unaware of this taboo opened his mouth, he would have closed it again when he became conscious of Edith, sitting in the wing chair, a tiny elegant presence, herself so concentrated. He would have been instantly silenced, content perhaps to watch for a few minutes that marvelously alive face in repose, to ponder the wide forehead framed in a casque of silver hair, and the great luminous eyes. Edith was not a beauty, but her face was arresting; it had so clearly been fashioned from within by strong forces of intellect, will, and emotion, some-times in conflict. And looking at Edith in this way, any stranger would have wished to know more, to know every-thing about her. But she was elusive and he might not ever have reached the heart of the mystery. She died in her early fifties—younger than I am now.

I saw her first when I was still in school at Shady Hill, in the same class with Bobby, her eldest son. Mrs. Kennedy like many other parents, like my mother, did some work at the school to help pay their children's tuition. She was sometimes in charge of a study hour and I found her inter-esting because she seemed rather different from anyone else around at that time. For one thing, she treated us at eleven or twelve years of age with a kind of amused respect we did not get from anyone else. She had style, and style was not exactly prevalent at Shady Hill where, because it was then still "an open-air school," both students and faculty often resembled bears, in their thick old sweaters and heavy boots. I liked to ask her questions because she gave very good answers, but she was not one of my teachers, and there was no real connection.

I came to know her several years later after I had gradu-ated from high school and gone to work at Eva Le Gallienne's Civic Repertory as an apprentice. The theatre had to be closed temporarily after I had been there for a year because Miss Le Gallienne was in a terrible accident; the furnace in her country home exploded and she was nearly burned to death, and had to take a year off as those burns slowly healed. My parents were spending that year in Beirut and it was decided that I would be allowed to study theatre in Paris on my own. I was nineteen. It happened that Edith

Kennedy was also in Paris that winter as companion for her
friend Mrs. Whitman. They had a small furnished apartment
on the Left Bank. I was subletting Willem Van Loon's studio
in the workmen's section of Montrouge, beyond the Porte
d'Orléans. Bobby, Edith's oldest, was studying at the Beaux-
Arts. It was the winter of 1931–32 at the height of the depression. I was very busy watching rehearsals of the Pitoëffs
and others, and going to the theatre to see Jouvet, Margué-
rite Jamois, Pierre Renoir, and many others in that especially
rich winter for theatre.

I did not see Edith often, but she was there, a kind of
friendly aunt who was perhaps keeping an eye on me without my being aware of it. What I remember is the gaiety of
that atmosphere. I can still see her and Mrs. Whitman doing
the Charleston to the absurd record "I Miss My Swiss, My
Swiss Miss Misses Me," and the gentle bubbling of the Sala-
mander which provided heat. But my entire being was in a
state of suspense all that winter, waiting for someone to come
over to Paris from New York. I am not going to rehearse the
dismal tale. For the first and only time in my life I had got
myself involved at nineteen with someone who proceeded
to use me dishonorably and badly. It precipitated not only an
emotional crisis, but after she did arrive in Paris, I found
myself getting into debt to support her. I was as weak as
only the unloved can be. And nothing in my life had prepared me to deal with crooks. By the time Edith Kennedy
intervened, I was close to nervous breakdown and five hundred dollars in debt, terrified of the future, not knowing how
to extricate myself.

Edith acted with surgical precision and helped me to
cut myself off, send home the devastating influence, and leave
Paris myself. She, who was by temperament extremely tolerant, compassionate, and large in her view of life where others
were concerned, could, when it came to the nub, act with

ruthless honesty. In this case, with a battered nineteen-year-
old involved, it can't have been easy; but it was necessary,
and she did it. She helped also by writing my mother, dread-
fully anxious in Beirut, to explain exactly what had happened, and why. (My father, rather typically, washed his
hands of the whole affair and never even asked me how I was
going to pay back a large debt!)

After that wise intervention, I did not come to know
Edith well until some years later, when my theatre company had failed, and I was back in Cambridge, slowly re-
covering and beginning to find my way as a writer. Then
she became for me an island of light, fun, wisdom where I
could run with my discoveries and torments and hopes at
any time of day and find welcome. There she sat, Jean
Christophe her briard dog at her feet, often listening to a
record, always open to life as it poured in and out of her
house. I note in my journal, "Supper with Edith: played
Beethoven while discussing, between records, the sense of
direction in an artist, also the failure of women to make
certain transitions from the personal. A man, Edith suggested, in the middle of an unhappy love affair might say,
'yes, it is all terrible, but I have just had a wonderful idea.'"

She had thought a great deal about men and women and
come to some definite conclusions. One was that men in our
time tended to root in women and that the opposite would
have been healthier. At the time I did not know enough to
disagree, but I sensed that whatever she said came from ex-
amined experience. I did not take it lightly, and it has stayed
with me, all of it. One of her geniuses was to set the purely
personal in a large frame, to distill out the essence, so that
even gossip became the field for philosophical speculation.
How often she said to me, "I am going to tell you something
strange—perhaps I shouldn't—but you are a novelist and
you have to know." She made interesting distinctions, one of

them being that between a character and a nature. She taught me an enormous amount, much that is so built in to my way of seeing things that I no longer remember that it originally came from a comment of hers. Most of all, she taught me to *think* clearly and hard about *feeling*.

One cannot have brilliant conversation without a wide frame of reference. Edith had had no formal education, but she had read enormously and listened to music passionately and critically all her life; so she could hold her own with, and stimulate, friends as various as Ernest Simmons, Edwin Cohn, George Sarton, Nancy Hale, or Elliot Carter. Yet she was never pedantic, used slang in a pointed and witty way, and could be extremely funny. For her, conversation was as important and as real as any other art. In that sense the atmosphere at 29 Shepard Street resembled one of the eighteenth-century salons in Paris, dominated as each was by a woman of charm and brilliance. But those women could afford to devote their chief energies to maintaining such an atmosphere, could take for granted servants, gardeners, a large house. Edith lived in a small shabby house, and had to work hard to make ends meet and to bring up her three sons.

Who was she? What had been her story? How had she become all that she was when I knew her? Little by little, in bits and pieces, I learned, though never all, never enough. As a child she had lived in her grandfather's house in Boston with her mother. Edith knew nothing about her father at all—"Every trace of him was destroyed"—and she was told never to speak to any man who might address her on the street, but to run home at once. Edith's grandfather, a retired sea captain, was the most important person in her childhood—"God," she said. He taught her Greek, and just before he died (when Edith was ten) he gave her an intimation of immortality which made a deep impression. A few minutes before he died, he suddenly sat up in his bed, arms

outstretched and an expression of radiant happiness on his
face and called his dead wife's name. Edith was a rationalist,
but she could never forget that look, nor what (perhaps) it
meant.

She described her mother as "brilliant, erratic, and hot-
tempered, with blazing black eyes, an icy-firm mouth, and a
beautiful narrow forehead." Sometimes when angered she
did not speak to little Edith for three days. Her mother never
went out except to concerts, but people did come to call,
Edith told me, and "the whole atmosphere of the room
changed when she came into it."

Three tales she told of her childhood stay with me. When
she was still in a baby carriage she remembered clearly
throwing her blanket out over and over again with determination. The second was an adventure. She and Ethel Lang
(who remained a good friend to the end) one day ran off
and got on a train all by themselves. When the ticket collector came and asked what station they wanted, Ethel
said, "What stations have you?" They listened while he read
off the list and chose Wakefield. Why Wakefield? I never did
hear the end of that tale. The third was about a journey to
Bangor for "a change of air." Her mother went by the fast-
est train, taking a great many books, but Edith begged to
go by boat, and this she was allowed to do, although her
grandfather hated and feared the sea, having seen many
people drown. "Aunty" (who later lived with Edith at Shepard Street) was delegated to chaperone her. Edith was terribly disappointed to find she had been given a first-class
cabin with a brass bed in it instead of a bunk. At four A.M.
they had to get up and transfer to a smaller boat for the last
leg of the journey. Aunty, feeling queasy, lay on a couch in
the ladies' room, so Edith was sent to the saloon alone,
where the only other person was a man with a black beard
reading the paper. The waiter brought little Edith a bowl

of pea soup, so thick that the spoon made roads in it. She couldn't face it (the boat was rocking in a sickening way at the pier), but she couldn't hurt the waiter's feelings either. Suddenly, when the waiter was out of sight, the bearded man got up and flung her soup, bowl and all, out the porthole. This wonderful man got off at Camden and was never seen again.

One gets the sense of a very determined, "cool" little girl who already observed life in rather a detached way, detached as children with hot-tempered mothers have to be. (Louise Bogan comes to mind.) About Edith's marriage I know very little. "K," as she called her husband, headed the Henry Street Settlement in Boston. His passion was rare books, and he indulged it, so there was never much money left for the household; yet quite often he announced casually that he was bringing six people home for dinner! I gather that the atmosphere at their table was icy-brilliant, and must have been uncomfortable at best for their three little boys. When I knew Edith she had been divorced a long time, and she almost never mentioned K. Once she said that he admitted that he had tried to break her spirit, and, when he did not succeed, "Well, that proves that your philosophy is stronger than mine. Hereafter I'll adopt yours." (Did he? one wonders.) She also told me more than once that when things were especially hard, she told herself, "At least I'm not married to K." Yet the divorce must have been devastating, for she spoke of going to Europe in a numb state—to Holland it was—after it had been settled.

It is hard to imagine how Edith made ends meet. But it is just here that she was so extraordinary, for never did one feel any sense of strain, never did the pinched financial straits show. How did she do it? When I knew her best in the late 1930s, Aunty had come to live with her. I presume this helped financially, but it was a nerve-racking burden

because Aunty was sentimental and demanding, always lurking about trying to decipher what was going on, sometimes
standing over Edith's bed at night peering down at her, apt
to be engulfed in depression and tears, always "trying to
help" in ways that only added a burden. There could be no
escape from her presence, and the house was very small.

I imagine the long days began early with breakfast for
Aunty. A few times a week one of a family of devoted West
Indians who worked for Edith when she needed someone
came to clean and tidy up, but often the beds were made,
dishes washed, by Edith herself. By around ten she usually
met with a group of young women who came to get her
criticism on their short stories, or in private session with a
single pupil. Edith sometimes took on odd jobs such as proof-
reading, but God knows when she found time. She fairly
often invited friends for lunch, and I remember with relish
the eggs Benedict that appeared for Lillian Hale (Nancy
Hale's mother) one day when I lunched there with her.
This meeting was typical of Edith's way of doing things.
She presented beautiful Lillian Hale to me as a present and
no doubt made us each feel privileged in the meeting. It was
a grand success. There was a real affinity, and Edith had
guessed there would be—across a generation.

By four in the afternoon the boys and their friends began to pour in and out. Bobby was engaged to be married
and might bring Gerta in for tea. Friends of all ages and
professions who might suddenly "need to see Edith" turned
up, expected or not. Records were played. Very possibly,
Edith had a dinner engagement, for she was very much in
demand.

But when she came home at eleven her workday was
just beginning. Then from midnight till sometimes four in
the morning she turned out slicks—worse than slicks—stories
for *True Confessions!* I was horrified at the waste when she

told me this, but the fact is that "serious fiction" is a chancy business. And she could turn out these potboilers mechanically and *know* they would sell. That she could be "literary" is suggested by the fact that she did sell at least one story to *The Atlantic Monthly*. So she managed, skating always on thin ice, never out from under. After her death Sean O'Faolain, who had known her in the days of the Henry Street Settlement, wrote to me, "She gave up a great, great deal for (I think) purely disinterested, unselfish love for her children, suffering many humiliations of the spirit for that." But of course it was worth it.

I have felt it necessary to speak of things Edith herself never spoke of because it was just this harsh reality of near poverty that gave the brilliance of her companionship, the art she brought to human relationships, an extra dimension of compassion that would have been quite different had not she herself experienced, experienced every day, what it is to have her back against the wall. It was also what gave her gaiety and joie de vivre a particular quality—Mozartian, I felt it to be, for Mozart too never had an easy time of it, God knows.

Once in a while I made sandwiches and a thermos of martinis and suggested that we go for a picnic. We had a favorite haunt near Concord where we spread a rug below a stone wall and looked out over pastures, the river, and some wineglass elms—a landscape of great gentleness and peace on a long summer evening. Being with Edith made everything become poetry, if poetry is what deals with essences in a wholly unponderous, undogmatic way.

Her sense of form explains her love of "occasions." Once she invited me with my parents to dinner to celebrate Mozart's birthday. Besides Edith, only Anne Thorp among our Cambridge friends succeeded in being equally my friend and that of both my parents, and I remember that evening

very well. My father was shy, and sometimes a little awkward on social occasions, and this time he was childishly
upset because he had worn white socks with his tuxedo—
why I cannot imagine! At any rate, he was humiliated by
this lapse. But Edith made him feel warm and at ease, and
soon he was talking brilliantly. Edith's two younger sons
were there. We listened for an hour or two to Mozart; we
talked; we all felt extremely happy, and the next day I had
a note from Edith:

> I have to tell you the aftermath of last evening, it was
> so rather lovely. When Eddie shut the door he came into
> the room and said to Fitz and me (sitting on the sofa),
> "Isn't she wonderful? Isn't she marvelous?" of your mother,
> and Fitz said, head in hands, "He's such a charming guy.
> Lord, he's a charming guy. He really does know what the
> score is," of your father.
>
> Both had shining eyes. Eddie in fact looked as though
> he had personally discovered your mother in the bulrushes
> or somewhere.
>
> In any case drinking a fine draught of the wine of
> Mozart with your family and you was one of life's really
> lovely minutes. I still feel it in all my veins.
>
> Yours for music and conversation,
> E.K.

Only Edith would have thought of asking us together,
and only Edith could have made the whole occasion flower
as it did. And she did this kind of thing for innumerable
friends. It was her idea of what life is about.

Yet the more I try to pin down her quality and her genius
(for it was surely that), the more elusive she becomes. She
was French in her insistence on mixing up all ages and
American in her ability to draw out people of very different
backgrounds. When I try to evoke the parlor at Shepard

Street, one occasion always comes to mind. Paul Child was there—he often came for weekends when he was teaching at Avon Old Farms. I was there, and I believe Elliott Carter. We were drinking and talking, perhaps, about Elliot's experience in Paris studying with Nadia Boulanger, when Eddie turned up with a friend of his, a hash-slinger in some joint, who happened to be a hot jazz expert. For a second it was a bit awkward. I wondered how Edith would ever manage to create some harmony out of such a disparate group. Small talk seemed the only refuge. Not at all! Edith skillfully turned the conversation to hot jazz and, before he knew it, the young stranger was holding forth on the subject in which he was expert, and we were listening, enthralled. Edith's brilliance had as much to do with making others able to be brilliant by creating an atmosphere where they felt appreciated and at home, as by her own wit and erudition. When one comes right down to it, she cared about people deeply, and about all kinds of people.

As a mother what she did was free her sons for what they wanted to do in life, never make claims or impose demands, be at their disposal in every possible way without ever being possessive. The fact that she had a rich life of her own helped, of course. I used to get angry when I saw Edith go down to the cellar to stoke the furnace while an able-bodied young man, strong enough to lift her in the air, as Eddie loved to do, sat lounging about in the parlor. But this was Edith's own stance . . . she wanted it that way. It was part of her belief about the relation between men and women, and perhaps also part of her pride. She did not want chivalry from her sons. She wanted growth and independence.

All this I had enjoyed for several years and had come to understand and cherish, as I went back and forth to Europe, as I wrote my first books, as I ran to tell her my "news" and to hear what had been going on in Cambridge whenever I

came home. But all these diffuse feelings of affection and
respect crystallized because of a strange circumstance. Even
now I cannot expose the raw nerve that was touched. Suffice
it to say that I turned up from Europe one afternoon bearing
a record and telling a tale of a harrowing experience of mine
without being aware that it would touch a deep wound of
her own. How could I know that the man of whom I had a
tale to tell had been her lover, and many years before had
betrayed her in tragic circumstances? How could I know
that she had not heard his name for years? How could I
know that the record we listened to, the one I brought with
me, was closely linked to that passion? All I knew was that
Edith was deeply moved, and even shaken. There was no
explanation, but suddenly Jean Christophe, the briard, lifted
his head and began to howl in a desolate way. I myself felt
seized by a strong current of emotion that had nothing to do
with me, but that carried me with it by its sheer intensity
and force. When the record was finished, Edith said, "Let's
go for a walk." It was not something we had ever done before, and again I sensed that she was compelled out of her
usual detachment. She had, for a half hour, lost her cool. We
walked, and she told me the whole story, including its bitter
end.

Nothing could have been farther from Edith's intention
than to involve me, nor from mine to become involved. But
what had happened, the release into the air of such passion,
was beyond her control. I was not alone in feeling its force.
A person who walked into the house some days later said
out of the blue, "This house is full of emotion." Edith laughed
a little ruefully when in the weeks to come more than one
man proposed to her under the same spell that had enchanted me into a kind of madness.

It was a perfect example of a seizure by "the muse," and

in the next months poems poured out of me, the poems that later were published as *Inner Landscape*. Like all such seizures that have little to do with the reality of a situation, I felt lifted up at first, for there is really no joy so great for a poet as to be tapped in this way, to be released into giving his gift in this way. And Edith was a marvelous muse, contemplative, listening with great attention when I ran in with a new poem, often making a succinct and helpful criticism, immensely *aware*, yet completely detached. She was the rock against which the waves broke into foam. And I could talk to her and discuss the whole strange absorbing experience, just as I always had with every momentous experience since I had known her as a friend. Nothing changed; yet of course everything had changed. It was a long autumn of rising tension that had to end somewhere. It did end in a cruel and haunting way by Edith's having a small stroke after Christmas. She fell downstairs and had a concussion. She was never again the person with whom I had walked through the Cambridge streets with Jean Christophe, driven by extreme emotion. That current had been cut off.

What Edith had done for me was to release the poet; her whole life can be seen, I believe, as doing this in differing ways for many, many men and women. To each of them she was a touchstone. One of the last to come into her life was Jonathan Howland, whom she helped, at first, with reading difficulties while he was still at Harvard. Jonathan went through medical school and is now a practicing physician. He measured his life, he once told me, as B.E. and A.E.— Before Edith and After Edith. Their relationship had a very special golden quality and it is good to think that an influence as propitious as Edith's had this final glow at the very end—a reciprocated light. I come back now to a letter written before our strange adventure because it suggests the

kind of exchange there was and also something about the
day-to-day stresses and joys of Edith's life. It is not dated. I
think it must have been in the summer of '37.

Dear May,

Your letter was very interesting, and made me very
sad too. It was a sad letter, but a good one for it showed
me that you have come to the idea that only by examination and re-examination can one be pared down to the
original center, where thought and feeling are always authentic. This seems like an egocentric method of breaking
out of the ego, but it's the only one I know of except that
of being put in a position of excruciating responsibility of
an incessant character, such as that of an army nurse back
of the front line, or in a position like directing terrific
traffic, without any previous experience.

I had a pretty busy weekend over the 4th, as I let El
go for two days, she was so tired by the heat, and I had six
in the family to cook for plus Aunty as mad as a robin.
Gerhart came up too and left you his love; he was exhausted and just sat and we talked late at night and he had
a nice time with Lilge, but he was too worn out by that
spell of New York Tophet to do anything. He thought of
you wistfully in Rockport, but he had such a paralysis on
him he could make no moves.

Paul is here drawing from a live model in town every
day and enjoying it. He has rigged up a studio down in
the cellar where it is delightfully cool, and Fitz got him
a fluorescent light at wholesale prices, which makes the
cave as if day were permanently there.

Johnny comes up about once in ten days for a German
lesson with Lilge, Nika has appeared again about her book
the Ms. of which I am now struggling with at all available
moments, and Aunty comes in about every ten minutes

regularly to be reassured. The Ulichs' cat killed and ate up
my largest bluejay which, though shrill, was beautiful as
anything, and I miss it as I sit at my bedroom window.
   My love to your Ma and Pa, and come see me soon.

Edith died in 1942, rather appropriately of an enlarged
heart. She has not wasted away; she had used herself up,
used every bit of her heart and mind and body to the limit
of what they could give. It had been a hard life, but full of
joys. And for those who were lucky enough to be a witness
even to a small part of it, full of magic powers. As I have
been thinking of her, thirty-three years after her death, what
I come back to is a poem I did not choose to include in the
Collected Poems. It has its place here.

IN THAT DEEP WOOD

What forests have you known,
How deep within the dark groves gone
And by what paths, alone?

People with green-drenched eyes
And silver casques of hair, what is
The region of your mysteries?

How the first passage to that wood?
Under what avenues of beeches stood
Where silence poured itself into your blood?

That wilderness is always where we meet
And a cool shadow falls across your feet
As if the air were boughs over the street.

Although the city bells are loudly clanging
Defeat and terror, although doom is ringing,
In that dark wood the silences are singing,

In that deep wood a green and airy light
Preserves from time, from change, from war, from night
The wild and secret powers of delight.

Part III

Grace Eliot Dudley

FIVE

Grace Eliot Dudley
Le Petit Bois

THERE ARE PEOPLE like wells; they become rarer and rarer in our times of diffusion and distraction, where the annihilation of distance imprisons rather than frees us as we go whirling round the globe, and a trip to Europe is no longer a long journey through limbo but a mere few hours' transit. There are houses that speak of intimacy and solitude, the secular equivalent of a very few churches, those one enters to know the spirit freed from all clutter and confusion, and given back to itself. Grace Eliot was such a person and she lived in such a house, for she had, by a stroke of luck, found the habitation that expressed her whole quality of being, that seemed like the concrete expression of a guarded inner life, all in depth.

I met her first in the vaguest and most ambiguous of circumstances, cut off in mid-Atlantic from all natural surroundings; and this suspended state of nonbeing was accentuated by the fact that she took to her bed on sailing and left it only on the last day. Mutual friends had suggested that I look her up, so I found my way from tourist to cabin class on the *Normandie*. Her cabin was lined in an elegant blond wood, but had no porthole. I soon discovered that she had no idea whether it was day or night; she slept and woke, and seemed to welcome my visits, and in that limbo between continents and between lives, while the ship's engines throbbed us toward France, we found ourselves moving into intimacy without any of the usual preliminaries. It was in May of 1938 and I was planning to spend a week in Paris to see my old friend Lugné-Poë, and then to go on to England. Why not drive down to the Touraine and spend a few days with her on my way? Well, why not?

So casually do momentous events take possession of our lives. There are very few unflawed relationships, very few one can look back on without a pang of guilt or frustration, of the too-little, or the too-much. But as I look back on my years of friendship with Grace, it shines like a snow crystal, unflawed and whole. To an amazing degree she had the ability to live in the moment, unhurried, unintense, tasting it slowly and to the full. She had achieved this art—for it is surely an art, and takes discipline, skill, and fervor, like any other art—not without pain. She had been, first of all, cut off from the normal life of a young girl by years of an acute thyroid condition at a time when medicine had not discovered any remedy except total quiet and isolation. For over a year she was not allowed to read a page that might make her feel anything, or to read a letter from a friend for the same reason. She lived from sunrise to sunset like a plant, breathing quietly and waiting for her life to be resumed. And she was a person who was meant to have a "life" in the richest sense. She was a granddaughter of President Eliot of Harvard, daughter of his beloved son Charles, the landscape architect who had the genius to design the park along the Charles, and who died cruelly young. Even her childhood had been deprived, since her mother, anchorless after this blow, fled to Europe with her children, and they were borne from city to city, rootless, cut off from the continuity of schools and friends, during their years of growing up.

At one time Grace had been the devoted secretary and companion of her grandfather; she had an acute intelligence and warmth of sympathy, and the inherited Eliot need to do something useful in the world. But fate continually thrust her back into herself, and she learned in middle life that a well is a very useful thing too; instead of having a job, or going "out," she created a world within to which people came, as to a well of peace and joy.

When she was able to get up again after her long illness, it was the beginning of the war, in which the man she loved was seriously wounded. After the war, when they were able to marry, the marriage ended in disaster after a very brief time. So the great lines of her fate were all tragic, all in concert to force her inward. What she made of this was not, as it might so easily have become, the melancholia of an invalid, a woman struck down brutally by circumstance, but a marvelous detached joy, a continual fountain of response to natural beauty, a sense of pure fun (her humor was like a shaft of sudden sunlight), and an ability to love people of every kind and from every social level for their own sakes, and in just the same astonished and delighted way that she observed and loved the old-fashioned roses in her garden. She never judged; she understood.

She was very much a part of "the world"—she greatly enjoyed visiting her chateau neighbors when she settled in the Touraine—but she was also, in some subtle sense, totally out of the world. And I think this may have been because she consciously created her life, each day, as if she were a poet creating a poem. This implies ruthless "cutting," of course, and constant revision, to bring the creation closer to the heart's desire. She said as much in one of her early letters to me; "If my *inner* place has shown itself, it is the result of years of pruning and clipping and snipping. In some ways I've shorn too much away and am rather bare in spots? You'd see this if you knew me better." But "bare in spots" strikes me as a completely false image. It was rather that as the life grew more and more rooted in the one place she loved, in France, it grew deeper. A well is not a brook, in constant motion, rushing down from mountains, bringing all sorts of things along with it—stones, rubble, and fresh water from the winter snows; the source of a well is deep in the earth. It is fed from within, and so with Grace, who had been given the right name. For finally in her middle life she walked into it—the perfect house, the place she was meant to find, the life she was meant to have. And there I knew her.

Deep in the Touraine, well under the layers of history, the Vallée Coquette retreats three miles from the village of Vouvray, with its hotels and advertisements of the wine-growers, past stone houses cut into the limestone hillside, past rows of beehives and whitewashed walls covered with roses, to the open fields and vineyards and to the Little Wood frequented by nightingales from which Grace Dudley's house took its name, Le Petit Bois. The old and the infirm, or the simply busy, do not go down to the village often; the valley is a community in itself.

When one climbs out on one of the steep little paths to take a look at the world, there is nothing to see but soft rolling fields covered with vines, the most delicate emerald green in spring, then indigo blue after they have been sprayed, and finally in autumn heavy with bunches of translucent pale-green grapes; wherever there is unplowed land,

there are patches of daisies, poppies, and bachelor's buttons,
scattered also through the occasional fields of wheat and
barley, giving an effect of stained glass. "Things will go
well for France," they say in these parts when the colors of
the flag are especially brilliant in the fields. A mile or so
away the river Loire, lazy blue ribbon, *"ce fleuve de sable et
ce fleuve de gloire,"* winds itself in and out of the changing
sandbanks and islands of poplars, a pomp of châteaux along
its banks. This is Ronsard's country, and Rabelais', and Péguy's.

But here in the Vallée Coquette the gods are not literary
or historical, but the living gods of the vine. There is really
only one topic of conversation from early spring to the
vintage: "Will it be a good year?" What complexities, what
nuances are involved in this passionately crucial subject,
what references to other years, going back well into the nine-
teenth century, what analyses of the weather—which must
be dry enough, be wet enough, be one thing at one season
and the opposite at another—what lingering over that mirac-
ulous 1948 when the town of Vouvray was decorated with
huge billboards advertising a "great" year!

"Surely you can stay for a bottle?" Madame Javarry's son,
Paul, disappears into the wine cellar without waiting for an
answer. The cellars, like some of the houses, are cut into the
limestone, a network of tunnels and caves, rock-cool on the
hottest summer day, insulated in winter, so the temperature
is equable. There the wine sleeps in the casks, stirring when
the moon is full and only a madman would bottle it; there
sleeps the god.

It's a late summer evening and we are sitting outside
under the veiled blue sky which makes the farmyard and the
apple tree, the beds of bright flowers by the house, the
canary cage hanging on the wall, and especially the barn,
where the last hay cart stands sagging under its load, look

faintly unreal like objects in a dream. Perhaps we are keeping Paul from unloading the hay? It's nearly nine and the
light is fading; they have not yet had supper. He gives us an
amused, slightly arrogant look from his bright, dark eyes and
says, "I'm my own master here." He stands there with the
bottle in his hands, he who can work and drink when he
pleases, looking like a clown of Picasso's blue period, for his
work clothes are dyed deep turquoise by the copper sulphate
which protects the vines.

Always there is a silence when the wine is poured. We sit
with the softly darkening sky, hyacinthine now, over our
heads, and slowly savor a wine of a deep gold, not too sweet,
but so perfumed that the taste stays long in the mouth,
"opens like a peacock tail," as the old wine books have it; we
sip and wait for the verdict, for each bottle is analyzed by
these connoisseurs like a work of art. "Not bad, eh?" Paul
says to his mother. "But it will be even better in another
year."

Until now there has been a slight tension, the tension of
the rite. Now we launch into conversation. Madame Javarry
has been up since daybreak working in the fields, and they
have not yet eaten, but this is the hour for talk. She embarks
on her favorite subject, the character of men versus women.
It seems that the canary, who had suffered from a mysterious
illness, died the other day. "And do you know what Paul
said when he found his sister crying? 'I'll get you another,'
he said." She pauses for dramatic effect, looking coldly across
at her son whom she adores. "There's a man for you! He
couldn't understand why Suzanne was furious," and she looks
across at him again with a tender, mocking smile, and shrugs
her shoulders. Her wisdom is salted with humor. She takes
nothing too seriously. And so one can talk to her about anything, about everything.

The talk turns inevitably to politics, to the state of France

—it is shortly after World War II. "We are paying," Madame Javarry says with perfect detachment, "for our greed. It's money, money, money. In the old days this was a village where everyone grew dahlias. People spent their spare hours growing dahlias, for pleasure, you understand, for the joy of it. We had wonderful shows, won prizes. But you'd never imagine it now, when every spare inch is plowed for a cash crop," and she shakes her head.

"You can't blame people when the cost of living is so high." Paul leans forward, intent on the argument.

Perhaps she has hit on part of the truth. But while we argue, I find myself thinking of Monsieur Hèrepin, who used to be a close neighbor, just over the wall. He died before 1940, but I vividly remember dropping in on him one evening like this. Monsieur Hèrepin, comfortable in slippers, his waistcoat unbuttoned over a worn khaki shirt, his trousers tied with a bit of string, greeted us with the formal grace of a Spanish grandee. He was just having his supper, and wouldn't we share it? There was only one chair, but this bothered no one; we stood. He knelt down before the open hearth, raked out two ash-blackened potatoes, opened them with his bare hands, salted them, and handed them to us with a flourish.

"That," he said with a smile, "is one of the best things you have ever tasted."

It was. It was also all he was having for his supper. But he was not in the least sorry for himself; he was delighted with his potatoes cooked *à point*.

It was this sense of life, this enjoyment of the simplest things, this gaiety at the marrow that made Grace feel at home here, more at home perhaps than in her native New England. The New Englander puts himself, too often, in the straitjacket known as "character," and Grace was a nature. Her nature was nourished at the roots by these people, by

this place, by Monsieur Hèrepin's potatoes, salted with humor and eaten with zest.

I think that when she first came there and discovered the
house, lost among the vineyards, it was its secretness, its atmosphere of a haven, a little aloof from the world, even the
intimate village world, that seized her heart like a passion.
And only later did she move out from it and discover all that
lay just outside the high wall and the iron gates. She saw it
first, as I did on that unforgettable spring morning in 1938,
standing like a ship or a fortress, high overhead, a glimpse
of a steep slate roof, a chimney angled up over the twenty-
foot wall of the garden. The rough dirt road, more like a
path, climbs sharply, and makes a hairpin turn to bring the
car suddenly face to face with the entrance, on a higher
level, with two square stone gatehouses and secretive shuttered gates with delicate ironwork decoration above.

On that first expedition it must have seemed like a fairy
tale, as if some sleeping princess lay locked inside, for it was
startling to come upon this elegant, small house, with the
dignified proportions of a miniature château (it had actually
been a hunting lodge before the Revolution) lost at the end
of the valley, as if it had been built in the first place—as perhaps it was—to shelter a secret life. And Grace recognized
it at once.

It was she and she alone who was surely meant to un-
lock the formidable gate with her key, to fling open the
French windows and step out into the enclosed garden high
over the vineyards; she who was destined to bring a piano
into the deathly stillness; she whose rich pure voice sang
out over the murmur of the many birds—a voice deeply
moving to those who loved her because some locked river of
passion in her flowed out through it and made the house
tremble; and it was she and she alone who must get up at
dawn and go out into the garden to transform it slowly

Le Petit Bois

from a wilderness into formal design, raking the sandy paths
between ovals and triangles of ivy radiating like spokes
around the sundial; planting the old-fashioned roses, *rose de
la mariée, la plus vieille rose du monde*, among the vegetables over the wall that divided the French formal garden
from a riot of flowers and vegetables just beyond it; she, in
the evening, who must swing back the heavy gate and go
walking out to find her neighbors.

Evening was the time for these casual visits, after the
long, rich, solitary day. Sometimes there was an errand to do,
to go in search of the pyramidal close-grained goat cheese
covered in a mold of green, which is the *spécialité du pays*, or
to Mademoiselle Penautot's for a rabbit. There was always
the feeling of climbing out into space, The World, from the
walled enclosure of the house. And on the way we looked
for wild orchids, or picked a bunch of wheat stalks, barley,
red poppies, and daisies to put on the mantel beside the little
seventeenth-century wooden Virgin which was the presiding
divinity of the house; Grace had found it on the very day
that she found Le Petit Bois, and always felt that it was
this little Virgin who had taken her by the hand and shown
her the way.

Mademoiselle Penautot sometimes came to do housework for us. Her black dress, ragged at the hem, and her
dark-gray apron were a familiar sight as she crossed the
fields. I remember the first time I saw her how astonished I
was when this peasant woman spoke of a neighbor's child
as "having great distinction," but I did not then know the
Touraine well. Mademoiselle Penautot spoke French like a
princess, and held her fine erect head like a princess too.

The first time I accompanied Grace on an expedition to
get a rabbit, it was quite late; we lost the path in the dusk
and had to wade up to the house through long unmown
grass. There was no light inside the one-room stone cottage,

but Mademoiselle Penautot heard our voices and came out
to welcome us, and to ask us in. In the dark we could just
make out the straw mattress covered with rough blankets in
one corner, the single straight chair, the two plaster statues
of saints on the mantel, and a few photographs. There was
nothing else. We felt shy before this poverty, but Mademoiselle Penautot was cheerful and at ease. Was there even a
candle?

Eventually we learned her story. She had been a nurse
in World War I, and had come home to find both her parents
invalids. So she stayed at home to nurse them, and when
finally they both died, she was middle-aged and all the
money gone. So Mademoiselle Penautot, with her ineffable
air, with her exquisite manners, did housework for the neighbors and raised rabbits.

As we drank Madame Javarry's wine while she and
Paul went on discussing the state of France, I thought of
these two—Mademoiselle Penautot and Monsieur Hèrepin,
and their sense of life, *quand même*, as Sarah Bernhardt used
to say. Money? Greed? No, I could not accept this as the
whole truth.

The poverty in the Vallée Coquette is hidden behind the
masses of roses which make the poorest house look opulent.
It is hidden under the grace and charm of the people, perhaps too hidden. It is easy to forget that here, as in every
remote country village, there are raw wounds buried just
under the surface. Once we came face to face with such a
wound; it was at an auction of the belongings of an old lady
after her death. There had been no love lost between this
dead maiden lady and the community, because she would
have no truck with it. Her forbidding house faced the church;
children coming out of Mass had thrown stones against the
tightly shuttered windows, but they had never succeeded in

probing the mysterious life behind them. Only after her death
the house was thrown open, and all its secrets paraded before the avidly curious, assembled villagers. We stood on the
outskirts watching the auctioneer, ludicrous in one of her
nightcaps, put up her corset, her best dishes, her lace curtains, her *pot de nuit*, and keep the bidders roaring with
laughter at his coarse jokes. Before him stood an elegant
baby carriage, upholstered in beige leather, its black hood
gleaming, like new—and perhaps fifty years old. As it stood
there, we waited, fascinated, to learn its story. Had the proud
old lady hidden a child long ago behind her lace curtains?

Finally the auctioneer leaned down in his ridiculous bon-
net and dragged out of the baby carriage, as if it were a
corpse, a huge beautiful baby doll. We could see the delicate white embroidered christening dress and the tiny gold
cross hanging on a chain round its neck. As he lifted it, the
china-blue eyes opened and stared at us blankly. There was
a second of silence. But the auctioneer's business was to keep
the crowd laughing, and this he was soon able to do, rocking the baby, pretending to cry, holding it up by one leg to
exhibit its lace underdrawers, and telling us that here was
the perfect baby, one who never wet its bed. There was
laughter and yet (did I imagine it?) it seemed rather em-
barrassed laughter. This last exhibit hit too close to the human heart, that heart that had fed itself for forty years on a
doll, the hard china-blue eyes that never responded to the
lullabies or tender words. The image was the image of
starvation.

When in the eyes of memory the Vallée Coquette looks
too much like heaven, I remember these casualties. But if I
were to choose one person as the symbol of all that Grace
Dudley loved, it would have to be one of those who survive
and triumph *quand même*. It would be, perhaps, Madame
Maillet. When we first knew her, she and her husband were

in charge of La Bellangerie, the big farm owned by the Château de Moncontour, which burned down during the last war. When we had walked across a mile or two of vineyards—the vineyards of the château—when we had opened and closed two or three separate gates to the farm and come out into its center, the great grove of oaks and the deep pond, we did not need to look for Madame Maillet. Invariably we could hear her loud voice somewhere about the place; perhaps she might be in the barn, milking, while she kept the other milkers in stitches of laughter. She was always in the thick of work, and always, it seemed, having fun.

She was a small woman with very dark eyes and then, at perhaps fifty-five, a deeply lined brown face. For she had had her share of trouble. After her husband's death she moved out of the Bellangerie, taken over by her son, and lived alone in a tiny house set against the hill near us. But she went over to her son's every day and worked as hard as ever. When we came back after the war, we had to knock at her door several times before we found her at home. It was the busy season and she did not get home to feed herself, her cat, and the rabbits till well after nine. But what a warm welcome we found when our knock finally received an answering shout! We sat in the tiny living room, drank homemade cordial, and heard the whole saga. For Madame Maillet is a heroine, at least among those who did not collaborate. The Germans left Vouvray pretty much alone—it was not a region where the Maquis were active—and Germans paid high prices for the poorest wine. So the vignerons here grew rich in the most patriotic way—by cheating their customers. The real suffering came from American and British bombers who flew over to blow up bridges and rather often missed their targets—at least the Americans, flying high in Fortresses, seem to have been singularly inept. So it was not altogether surprising to find that an equivocal attitude toward "the

allies" was prevalent in the valley. One of our richer neighbors told us he thought it plain stupid to resist; "we knew
the Americans and British would come eventually. Why stick
one's neck out?" He spoke with amused condescension of
Madame Maillet's courage as one might speak of a foolhardy child.

It was foolhardy, if you like, to do what she and her
family had done. For when a British bomber crashed in their
fields, the fire could be seen for miles around and it was
certain that the Nazis and Vichy police would be there in a
matter of minutes. But somehow the Maillets, working as a
team, managed to extricate three members of the crew and
to hide them in the woods. Madeleine, the daughter, and our
special friend in the family, ran in her nightdress, barefoot
through the stubble and prickly bushes, leading them to a
ruined tower deep in the woods. There they were secreted
while the farm was searched, and searched again. Finally
the British were brought into the house and hidden in a cupboard. Every day the Maillets were in real danger—if any
of the crew had been discovered the men in the family would
have been shot without trial. Alas, there are always inform-
ers. One such from a village nearby was responsible for the
death of a farmer who had sheltered a French deserter from
the Vichy army. After the war this informer got six months.
Only when Madame Maillet told this story was there dry rage
in her voice. Injustice to others could bring the fire to her
dark eyes, but it was typical that she brushed aside with a
shrug of her shoulders and a laugh the fact that she herself
was considered a fool by the village and had never had any
recognition for what she had done.

I came to understand what the word "neighbor" means
from sharing now and then the last years in Grace's life at
Le Petit Bois. Nothing could keep her away, even when she
was dying—she must get "home" each summer—and I saw

the discreet affection which she had always inspired become
something more. We could no longer walk out in the late
summer evenings among the vines. Now the neighbors came
to us. They came, one or another of them, every day. They
came after their work in the fields and vines, too late often
to dare to pull the bell at the closed gate. They came to
leave a basket with a cheese, a chicken, or a dozen eggs, and
always a few flowers. They came, those who could, in the
late morning to ask for news, deeply concerned, yet wonderfully sensitive about never asking too much. And sometimes,
when Grace had gone to sleep, I stole out after dark, and
went to Madame Javarry or to Madame Maillet to ease my
heart. In those hours and days of anxiety, the barrier of
strangeness went; we were simply friends.

And from the village of Vouvray, Marie de Lestanville,
Grace's one intimate friend, she of the great grave blue eyes
and English beauty (she always reminds me of my mother)
came often, walking or bicycling up the long dusty road, to
bring us comfort and joy.

In the years she had lived there, a stranger from a foreign land, Grace had slowly woven herself into the fabric
of life in the valley. She had learned the traditional ways of
receiving and giving in the Touraine. For instance, one day,
the day of the "Basilique," I was dispatched to the city of
Tours nine miles down the river to get a series of pots of
basil to leave at the doors of all Grace's friends. On this day
the pavements of the city are covered with a green sea,
basil clipped to make fat rounded bushes, pots of every size,
for every purse, for it is St. Basil's day, the fourteenth of
June.

She was lying in the cool salon as in some great airy
bower; she was very ill. But she did not forget Basil's day,
and her voice grew warm with its old resonance as she gave
me my directions.

This visit was the last time I saw Grace. When she died the next year, I was not there. But the neighbors all wrote to tell me what they could of that last summer and of the funeral, and I heard it again from her beloved sister Ellen, who was able to fly over and to be with her at the end. I see, as if I had been there, the little procession winding down through the vineyards on the rutty road, a procession of friends on foot, laying a friend to rest. I see the modest hearse, "a second-class hearse," drawn by a single horse, the black plumes on his head, and the great wreath of laurel and ivy from the garden lying on the coffin. It was surely good that Grace could die here in the place and among the people her heart had chosen. Such a death takes its place there among the days and the seasons, and will be referred to in the years to come as perhaps, "the year when Madame Dudley died," with the inevitable afterthought, "not a great year for the wine."

Grace is not there, but Le Petit Bois has not changed. Some years later I went back, opened the heavy gates, unlocked the door, and walked into the silence. I had been afraid, afraid that all I would hear would be a great cry of absence, that the house would seem too empty to bear. Instead, it seemed full of peace, of Grace's own presence, all alive and still, all in depth, and I felt the silence like a balm. I had come here first at a time of turbulent emotion in my own life, and Grace had been the healing balm. Those days came back in a quiet flood: how I sat at my desk in a window upstairs and looked down over the sandy paths of the garden and out over the vineyards, and how often I heard Grace's voice singing as she bent to transplant some seedlings or while she clipped a hedge; how we came together in the evening after the solitary days, and threw a *javelle* of dry vine-twigs on the fire and watched it blaze up in the little "cosy room," where the Virgin looked down at us from the mantel and I read the day's poem; how after Emilienne, the servant, had left in the evening and we were enclosed in the private world of the house and the garden, a different rarer silence began. And how, late in the evening, as the moon rose, we sometimes stole out to listen to the nightingales in the Little Wood.

"There are people like wells," I wrote at the beginning of this chapter. The places such people create are full of blessing, and it does not, as I learned when I went back, die with them. It goes on, just as a work of art goes on living and nourishing. I came to the house with someone who had never known Grace, and this was the proof. For this friend who came to the house at a time of turbulent emotion in her life as I had done long before, recognized the quality of presence, not absence, and drank deep of the balm.

—May Sarton

Alice, Haniel, and Tony Long

SIX

Alice and Haniel Long
The Leopard Land

I SAW IT FIRST in December of 1940, the high plateau among the red and purple mountains, where Santa Fe lies in a wide open bowl; a city built of adobe, traversed by mountain streams, lined with cottonwoods; a city that, though a capital, has kept the air of a village (there is no railway station) and spreads out onto foothills covered with pinyons, tawny earth dotted with these small dark pines so that it looks like a leopard skin—the leopard land. Then, in December, the earth looked blood-red among the patches of snow, and the mountains, luminous and bare, looked like mountains on the moon. I was unprepared in every way, unprepared for the air itself, seven thousand feet up, thin and dry so there is a bubble of physical excitement in one's chest; unprepared for the huge bare landscape that reminded me of Chinese paint-

ings and of Northern Spain. For my target had been a friend
rather than a city, a friend I had never seen, but one who had
written me a letter when my first novel came out, Haniel
Long, the poet.

This was a year of discovery. I had been until then ori-
ented toward Europe, to the old roots in Belgium, to the
friends I had made in England as a young writer; I had gone
over every spring since 1936 to stay until late autumn. In the
interval two books of poems had appeared, and my first
novel. The fall of France in that terrible May of 1940, the
excruciating months that followed, made me restless, made
me long also to be doing something useful. So I sent out a
hundred or more letters to colleges all over the country,
offering my services to speak of poetry (the title of one of
these lectures was "The Spirit Watches"; another, "Poetry
as a Dynamic Force"). I asked that they put me up for a few
days and pay me twenty-five dollars. These letters were
really rather like messages in bottles sent out to sea, but the
amazing thing was that fifty colleges scattered here and there
did respond.

I had a new Mercury convertible given me by my father
and fifty dollars a month allowance, and I set out in the
autumn to drive south, then west. There were gaps between
engagements when cash ran low, but time was my luxury; I
could settle in to some town where I was a stranger (as once
for ten wonderful days in Eureka Springs, Arkansas) and
write the poems that sprang out of my first encounters with
Charleston, Monticello, New Orleans, the windy golden
plains of northern Texas.

Between these experiences, the more intense because I
was alone, there were the sociable intervals at the colleges.
In the course of those months I was coming of age as an
American at long last. And now in December, after speaking
at Colorado College, I drove down a winding dirt road into

Taos late at night, and then on the next day to an appointment for tea with the Longs, who had kindly arranged for my stay in Santa Fe over Christmas.

Like many Santa Fe houses, theirs was secret, a blank adobe surface from the outside, the large garden concealed behind a surrounding wall. But, once inside, I was at ease, in my element. Was it the high ceilings reminiscent of houses in Europe, or the dark Victorian furniture? Or the abundance of books and magazines on the low table by the fire, and the many bright objects—jars of flowers, plants on the window sill, something gay, lively, and intimate against a background of such solidity? Or was it Alice and Haniel Long themselves, who at first sight resembled an early American painting—he, spare, tall, with lean, high cheekbones and a wide mouth; she, plump as a tea cozy, with a light child-voice and soft vague hands, altogether absurdly like a dove? Or was it all of these together, and the two people who welcomed me to their home as an old friend? I know that I felt I had come home after a long journey. And I knew it wholly when I heard Haniel's laugh, that tart, heady laughter that cut right down to the marrow of things, while I poured out my experiences of the last weeks, and drank cups and cups of tea.

I remember coming out in the early December dark and standing a moment under the immense sky, the hills lying at the horizon like great sleeping animals, and felt that tremor of something like fear which seizes one at the brink of major experience: out of the strangeness that opens a new layer in the subconscious, a homecoming—homecoming into a new world, an ancient world, the world of poetry for me.

Sometimes a place and a person together fuse in the imagination and seem forever one. So it had been for me at Vouvray with Grace Dudley, who had opened the heart of France for me there. So it was to be now. With a word, more often a silence, Haniel opened the experience of Santa Fe. At first it was a hundred small concrete things: it was a walk down among the pinyons along a dry arroyo, where we suddenly came upon six bright bluebirds in a single tree; it was a piece of winter jasmine he brought me from his wall and I knew suddenly how far south we were in the high winter air; it was his naming the flowers, the stars, the trees like some local god: chamisa, the pink tamarisk so feathery and light, the gingerale tree (a tree hung with seeds that sizzle in the wind), later the roses of Castile, flame and gold; it was the mountains, the Sangre de Cristo, those old kneeling elephants, whose snows reflect the sunset, and the cruel Sandias near Albuquerque; it was his reference to the Acequia Madre, the mother stream that feeds all the gardens in the city, that made me suddenly realize that water in this dry land is like blood, the stream of life itself, never to be spilled carelessly; it was his sense of communion with his Spanish neighbor Herrera who would come in the spring to plow the garden; it was the Chinese restaurant—he took me in through the kitchen to meet the family who have become the friends of everyone in the city—where we talked and drank tea and Haniel spoke of teaching and said he did not think I should do it full-time "You must stay teachable as long as possible"; it was introducing me to his friends, the painters Agnes Sims and Dorothy Stewart, who became my friends; it was, that first night, his taking me to Lura Conkey's warm welcome to a strange guest (from her wide portal I could look down on the twinkling city, fairy-bright in the crystal air); it was finally the way in which one goes to see a dance at one of the pueblos, casually, yet with ceremony. It was a certain ease and intimacy with the whole complex of a place that felt like home to me because, as in Europe, one is in touch here with vertical time. In a few hours one moves about among the centuries, from sixteenth-century Spain, back five or six hundred years to a pueblo, or forward to the creak of my neighbor's well in the early morning, when I had settled. later, on Canyon Road. At the center of all this Haniel opened for me the door into the silence, "like the old roar of ocean in a seashell," as he said.

From the beginning, from that first night when we stood out in the dry cold under the brilliant winter sky, and I felt the tremor of recognition, Santa Fe was to be for me the place of Poetry. I would go back over and over again, always in fear and trembling, as if to a source—would the source still be there? But one of the reasons it always would be was the presence of these two remarkable natures who had created of their differences a marriage as whole as the two "Philips" in a double almond. A good marriage is a source, one of the deep sources, of poetry for those who witness it, and although Haniel was a true poet, no poem of his reaches (to my mind) the depth and the intensity of his creation as a human being and in his personal relationships. Are true marriages rarer than good poems? I sometimes think they are.

The Longs lived like Chinese philosophers, in close touch with the seasons. They communicated peace partly because of their sense of the immediacy of the moment. "What do you think Haniel was doing when I came back from church?" Alice wrote me one February day. "He was in white overalls pruning the fruit trees. There was a soft downy uncertain snow falling. That is the first sign of spring." And in March, "We woke up this morning, Sunday, with the sky overcast and the smell of moisture in the air and wet earth. It was half raining and half snowing. Jackie and Haniel did things in the garden around the yellow jasmine—it is blooming at the base, the crocus and the green tips of hyacinth are cracking the earth. They do have such energy. The birds are busy with

the detail of their life." Alice had the eye for essentials of a
Chinese poet and her letters brought me always right back
as if I had never left; "It is so lovely here just now. The
cherry tree is lacy white and the wild plum and the pink on
the peach coming out of its fur cover. My summer clothes are
airing on the line and our overshoes are going back into the
box."

And in May, "Haniel's chief joy are the peonies. He just
brought in the first one. A delicate shell pink." Or in another
year in May again, "It was a typical spring day of driving
clouds, showers, and bright sun. Lilac purple everywhere,
and bright green cottonwoods in purple canyons." What
these letters evoke, like the scent of pinyon smoke from the
chimneys when one walks out at night in Santa Fe, is the
poetry of domesticity, the exact detail, all that makes a good
cook and a good poet: "I tried a receipt for vichyssoise, with
half celery put through the sieve with the potato and sautéed
the onions first in butter. It was very delicate."

This preoccupation with the essences of things implies,
of course, the ability to choose what is important and to
shut out everything else ruthlessly. In their life together,
Haniel's work was important, and the fact that he was highly
nervous and tired quickly; the continual nourishment of their
intimacy through all the daily and seasonal rituals and joys
was important; friends were important. When I knew them,
they did not have financial problems, though they lived with
exquisite frugality. But Haniel had taught for twenty years at
Carnegie Tech in Pittsburgh in the English department. They
were not remote from ordinary human struggles; they had
experienced them, one felt. They had one son whom they
treated with respect, and freed early to become himself:
grandson of a missionary, son of a poet and teacher, Tony
Long began his career as a teacher, first in Socorro, New
Mexico, and later in Jamaica. Haniel said in a poem,

. . . And who then or who now
Knows whether knowledge and peace are to be striven
    toward
Or a place prepared by us for them to come to?
With Navajo marauding, and the drought lurking,
And the slaves and peons restless and resentful,
It was a good question to go to sleep with
For the Spaniard facing the terror of his New World;
As it still is, for you or for me tonight,
Sleepless between our future and our past,
Sleepless between our furies and our demons.°

    And in this last book of poems there are references to
Haile Selassie°° ("You take your place among those shades
of grief / With which all men have dealings inwardly"), to
the fall of France, and to the death of Roosevelt. From their
island of peace the Longs reached out to the world around
them. They could move from a centered innocence into the
most complex problems. Yesterday, as I was going over old
letters and re-reading Haniel's poems, I found myself moved
to tears to find the word "democracy" (a word that has almost lost its savor) treated again as he treats it in a poem
called "The Law."°°° I quote the two final stanzas:

> Eating and drinking are
> No pleasure till we know the terms
> Of hunger. So the law
> That from the angel reaches to the worms:

> Greatest the joy that will
> Be ushered in by greatest pain.
> Grow and inflame me still,
> Democracy; sweeten in me again.

° "May Your Dream Be of the Angels," from *The Grist Mill* (Santa Fe.,
N.M.: The Rydal Press, 2d ed. revised 1946), pp. 16, 17.
°° "I Come for Justice," *ibid.*, p. 19.
°°° Haniel Long, in *The Grist Mill*, p. 27.

Pain is never very far off; Alice and Haniel had their full measure of it in the years to come. He was to suffer two excruciatingly painful operations on his eyes, and then to go partially blind after all.

I should like, before speaking more personally of the Longs, to go back for a moment to that winter of 1940, to my first experience of the Indian dances. Many times in later years I went to the San Felipe Pueblo with Alice and Haniel, for the spring corn dance fell very close to my birthday, and we made a rite of celebrating it together. But I went there on that first Christmas Eve, when all was still new and strange to me, without them. Dorothy Stewart, my friends the Asplunds (with whom I was boarding), and I set out after eleven, in a blizzard, to drive for forty miles on a dirt road through what seemed to me a trackless and terrifying wasteland. Not a light, not a sound. About halfway the mud became so deep and thick, it was like soup, and driving became more like swimming. It was one A.M. when we finally arrived in the dark village, saw the lighted church down a muddy path, and stopped the car. At once we could hear the steady throbbing beat of the drums, an ancient primeval sound to come from a Christian church. But it did not seem incongruous once we had gone in, so primitive and fresh was the atmosphere of the place, the dirt floor, the rough whitewashed mud walls where garish reproductions of the Stations of the Cross had been pinned, and, above all, the brightly painted wooden pulpit which was, that night, inhabited by a radiant crown of small Indian boys, peeping over the edge like seraphs. It was a little odd to glance from the drummer, splendid in his red shirt and high boots, to the quite ordinary Virgin in pale blue and crowned in paper flowers who looked down at him from the altar, and looked down too on the lines of Indians standing against the walls, wrapped in brilliant blankets, the men carrying papooses, their dark eyes the only thing that moved.

We and the Franciscan priest in his medieval brown habit and sandals were the only Anglos present, and he was not an outsider, since he was to say Mass later on; these strange sheep in Indian clothing were actually his flock. It was half past one; the dances were just beginning. As we found places against the wall, the drums were coming to a crescendo, and about to move into the intricate and subtle beat for the first dance. The earth vibrated with them; one could feel the beat through one's chest and down into the earth through the heel bone, that life-giving, centering beat that in the years to come would mean so often for me the waking of the buried source. But I was hearing it then for the first time, and it seemed powerful but strange, and I myself lost in some fantastic dream to which I had no key.

Hypnotized by the rhythm they carried, I looked first at the dancers' feet—the men's in soft leather boots the color of terra-cotta, and the women's, delicate and small, in white. The dancers carried pine branches in one hand, a gourd rattle in the other, and as the pattern formed, the deep rich voices of the men broke into a chant, the penetrating song that swells and dies away, over and under the steady beat of the drums. The first dance was a humorous one, making fun of the Navahos, which explained why the men had on what looked like long woolen underwear with bells at the knees and elbows. No one smiled; so I did not understand this until afterward, when Dorothy Stewart explained it to me. She at least looked as much a spirit of the place as did the Franciscan or the Indian boys in the pulpit, her dark eyes and exquisite profile set off by a wide-brimmed Stetson, her body enveloped in the heavy blanket coat (white in the somewhat grimy way a sheep is white, and banded in broad

stripes of green and red) that she always wore on such occasions, on her feet soft leather shoes with silver buttons
like those of the dancers. Somehow her presence that night
added one more element to my early appreciation of the complex quality of Santa Fe—a place where people can live as
they please, one of the few places in the United States where
eccentricity is cherished, because perhaps, people are either
overwhelmed by the sheer grandeur of the landscape or are
forced to become strongly individualized characters.

The final dance was, that night, the great moment for
me, for it was my first sight of the heavy black fur head-
dresses of the buffalo dancers, of the light antlered deer
heads, and the antelope, beige-colored with bobbing white
tails, who moved with quick stylized gestures, all like some
myth being reenacted before my eyes, some return to the
deep unconscious where animal and human life make their
close connections. I felt it again at Lascaux in the cave paintings of bulls, the worship and reverence, and the deep
strange excitement. But I was unprepared for the interlock-
ing of the myths, for at the end of the buffalo dance, the
animal dancers go one by one to make obeisance at the altar;
the buffalo, the deer, and the antelope bow their wild heads,
and kneel before the centuries-later image of compassion, the
Catholic Virgin in her blue cloak.

When I finally got into bed at four A.M. in my whitewashed adobe room in the house on Canyon Road where I
was living with the Asplunds, I had an intimation of one of
the reasons why Santa Fe was to become such a beneficent
place for me. It is a place of reconciliation, a place where
peace has been made, between the Anglos, the Spanish-
speaking people, and the Indians, between two religions each
still strong and powerful in its own right. The Franciscan
priest, Fray Angelico Chavez, a poet himself, watched the
dances with respect; just as the Indians who stayed on for

the Mass on Christmas morning would accept his vision of
the Divine Order with respect. There in the muddy, primitive church it seemed as if the loving regard for one another which Haniel Long's whole life expressed—which is
also the renewing myth of Christmas—was brought home to
me. I remember wondering when I woke up if it had all
been a dream.

But it was not a dream. It was a reality, and I was to
receive its impact many times after that, and consistently
feel compelled to try to get it into poetry. The last time I
saw the spring dance at that same pueblo, San Felipe, was
with the Longs, on May 1, 1945. It was near the end of the
war, and the dance was being danced, so Haniel told me, in
honor of all the boys from the pueblos in the armed services.
I remember how Western he looked, in his black Stetson and
leather jacket, as he talked about it, how good it was to think
that those boys scattered over Germany and in the Pacific
knew that on this day their families would be gathering
green branches, and repainting their houses, and their fathers
shutting themselves up in the kiva for three days in preparation for the great dance of renewal and fertility.

We drove through the mountains-on-the-moon wasteland
so familiar to me now, until we came to the fresh green valley along the Rio Grande where, just under the high cliffs of
a mesa, the pueblo I had not been able to see on that dark
Christmas Eve in the snow sits, brown and gold and beige
under the brilliant blue sky. Again, as we stopped the car,
we could hear the drums in the Plaza; I ran toward them
while everyone laughed at my impatience, for the dance had
begun at eleven (it was now four) and I was only showing
my Anglo sense of time. Many times a group of a hundred
dancers, following the tall shaking banner that leads them
like a flame, had already danced their way in and out of the
Plaza, and made way for a new group. In the middle, as al-

ways, a closed circle of old men—dressed magnificently in
red and purple shirts, white full trousers tucked into high
burnt-sienna boots—chanted, their voices rising amazingly
clear and sweet in the sunny air.

Always at first there is so much to see that one is not *in*
the dance. All around the Plaza, a great open square of bare
earth, surrounded by the low geometrical shapes of the
adobe houses that give it form, and even on the roofs, sit
Indians and their guests wrapped in bright cotton blankets;
the children have new dresses, their faces shine, and they run
around like rabbits, eating ice cream cones. Always there are
several dogs, winding in and out, or lying down casually
among the moving feet. Only after seeing the dance about
three times over does one begin to be part of it, to understand the shape, and feel the rhythm in one's bones like the
pulse of one's own blood.

And there is always a moment finally when one looks up
from the low adobe houses, the sunbaked hard earth of the
Plaza, and the brilliant figures, to the immense sky overhead.
And that is the good moment when one begins to be part
of everything.

At about five that May day we saw the last dance begin.
Haniel said we could tell it was the last dance because, instead of disappearing behind the houses, the group finishing
off had gone to sit in a long line on one side to watch the
second group come in. One of the devils, Koshari, put on a
small impromptu divertissement for this audience; he pretended to be a woman, chose one of the men from among
the watchers and teased him into a humorous dance. The
Indians on the sidelines suddenly began to laugh with high
sweet voices like birds; it was lovely to hear them. But
Haniel said he had never seen them dance so devoutly at San
Felipe as on that day at the end of the war.

As the second group finished, the old singing men gathered

round the statue of San Felipe who had been placed in a bower of green branches to watch the ceremony from the beginning (again that meeting of the myths in amity and reconciliation); they made a circle round him and knelt, while the dancers formed in two lines, holding up their pine boughs to make him a passage. Lifted in his bower, the saint was carried shoulder high, preceded by the governors of the pueblo, dignified old men carrying canes. The drum beat a fast, gay beat, and attending Indians shot off muskets and shouted—a traditional reference to the sixteenth-century conquistadors. As they came to the end of the Plaza, the two lines converged and were joined by the public, all of us together following the progress of the saint up the narrow path to his church. Then—it was a most extraordinary musical transition—they were suddenly singing sacred Catholic music as they bore him home.

We saw the very end from our picnic place on the bank of the muddy Rio Grande, under some cottonwoods. Up till now it had all been communal, but the final rite is private and individual. The dancers come one by one, when the spirit moves them, and lay in the stream the branches they have carried all day through the dance, to bless the other pueblos, on their way to the sea. And soon the river is full of green. Finally each dancer strips and bathes alone.

Erna Fergusson, friend of the Longs, and authentic writer on the Southwest, for she is the daughter of pioneers, had provided a sumptuous picnic for us all. She told us, I remember, that her mother had been on the first train that ever ran from Albuquerque—on her way to make the Grand Tour of Europe. We were joined by a Chinese anthropologist who could hardly speak English, but who ate a great deal, and took photographs, and then sang in his high light voice several Chinese poems for us; Haniel recited two poems of Ruth Pitter's, and we were very happy.

As we drove home, it was nearly dark, and far off over the mountains great flashes of summer lightning illuminated the sky.

These were ceremonial occasions, the celebration of the changing seasons, and each had its intimate equivalent in Haniel and Alice's garden: the setting out of the young lettuces from the cold frames, the planting of the bean poles and raspberry canes, and the day when Herrera would come with his "dappled horses" and "bright plow" to do the spring plowing. There was the ceremony of water, when for one day in the week the Acequia Madre could be diverted into the small geometrical channels that nourished Haniel's garden. There were the ceremonies of homecoming, as friends returned from the war. One evening in April of '45, I was invited to supper to welcome Fray Angelico Chavez, home after a year as chaplain in the Pacific. I had seen him once before, in the church at San Felipe, on Christmas Eve five years before. Then he had worn the brown habit and sandals of the Franciscan, and it was strange to see him now in an officer's uniform. He brought out a sheaf of poems to read to us, and I learned that he was one of the poets with whom Haniel had founded a small cooperative publishing house, Writers' Editions, with the idea of decentralizing the publication of poetry, of making each region a center in its own right.

One of the vivid impressions I brought back with me after that first trip across the country in 1940 had been the vast areas uncelebrated in poetry; how, as a traveler, one longs for the celebrations, for the expression of man's relationship to his country, to his region. What Willa Cather did for the pioneers of Nebraska needs to be done again and again—in Arkansas, in Texas, in South Dakota. Without the tender evocations, the songs, a traveler feels loneliness in the air,

something raw, not yet humanized. Seeing the great golden
stretches of Texas, for instance, he longs for the words that
might express his feeling, for the sense that someone here
before, some dweller in all the immensity, felt what he feels,
and made a touchstone. It was partly this that had moved
me to write a whole series of poems on American landscapes,
and it was this same need that impelled Haniel and his
friends to organize what they called "The Poets' Roundup,"
a yearly occasion before my time, when local poets gathered
to read their poems, stepped into the ring as cowboys do, or
as Welsh bards do, to vie with each other in friendly competition.

And it was especially suitable that within this group of
poets, one should be a Catholic priest. For it is not only the
presence of the pueblos that give a sense of vertical time to
this part of the world. It is also the presence of the Catholic
Church at its most simple and tolerant.

The people of the tiny mountain villages and the small
isolated fertile valleys are peasants, for whom local saints
are as present as living people, requiring the same tact, love,
and forbearance as do all personal relations. When one walks
into any village church, one walks back in time three or
four hundred years. The continuity creates peace. I think
especially of that loveliest example of these, the church
called Sanctuario. Built of adobe, of the earth itself, as all
these churches are, it looks like a fortress. Before it stand two
immense cottonwoods, their branches intertwined, their roots
nourished by a mountain stream; so the church is blessed by
water, and indeed this water has the reputation of healing
and there are ex-votos, crutches, and braces hanging on its
walls. Inside, it is whitewashed, the floor of earth, but the
impression created within this austere frame is of a flowering gaiety and joy. The altar is covered with bright paper

flowers and Christmas tree decorations, used as if they were
"everlastings." There are many *Santos*, the wooden carved
figures of saints made by journeyman artists or some pious
local woodcarver, examples of a folk art with spiritual grandeur, for they are filled with the implacable Spanish sense
of the place of pain in life.

In all these churches, the crucified Christ is austere and
terrible. There is nothing of the saccharine pretty-prettiness
of many modern plaster images that have, alas, already often
taken the places of the *Santos*, even in New Mexico. But here
at the *Sanctuario*, the awe-inspiring Christ is surrounded by
love, flowering in the shape of innumerable saints, and especially the famous el Santo Niño de Atocha on horseback, who
must continually be given new pairs of shoes for, legend has
it, he wears them out doing good deeds secretly at night.
These saints have many different suits of clothes, as do the
beloved Virgins in all the little churches, clothes that are
changed as the church year proceeds. But many of these
dresses and coats and boots go back to the conquistadors;
Joseph or Philip may wear a great plumed hat, velvet dou-
blet and hose, and the rich cape of the Spanish grandee.

The Church provides its own outdoor festivals, not too
unlike the Indian dances, for the same reverence and casual-
ness accompany them. On Corpus Christi the Host is carried under its purple-and-golden canopy and, preceded by
little girls in white throwing rose petals, is moved awkwardly along the rough dirt roads to some flowered altar in
front of the poorest of adobe houses. This is the Church at
its best, the Church with which a nonbeliever can feel himself reconciled, because it keeps beauty and ceremony alive
through belief, and nourishes the heart.

Whether one is a pueblo Indian, rooted in an ancient
communal life and steeped in its traditions and rituals, or a

Spanish-speaking Catholic from a village, or a modern city dweller on holiday, there is something in this landscape and its whole atmosphere that transcends the "picturesque" entirely, and makes austere demands on the inner self. For it is a landscape stripped down to essentials, the bare bone of mountain and rock and the extreme clarity of light upon them. Living with it one lives in the presence of ultimate questions, and there is no escaping them.

If one is as sensitive to such things as Alice and Haniel Long were, it may be necessary, in order to live there permanently, to protect oneself, to tame the sometimes overwhelming space and silence, in the shelter of a house, or a garden, where intimacy and humanity may flourish and feel at home.

No doubt Haniel's earthy, flavorsome humor was one of his defenses or shelters, a defense against overexposure of the nerve, both from his physical surroundings (let anyone smile who has not seen one of the summer storms come towering over the high peaks to crack the sky apart) and from the invasions of personal emotions. As Alice said, when a close friend of theirs died. "Haniel takes his going very hard. You poets have such a time with the tangent relationships."

He could react quickly, and with laughter. In one of his last letters, dictated, I find this characteristic passage: "Francis Fergusson's book on the theatre (now being read to me by a Harvard boy out here on vacation) contains a smart aleckism which made me really laugh. He quotes an absurd passage from Nietzsche, about Wagner's *Tristan*, 'Is there a soul so dead that he does not feel himself dissolve in the primitive womb of darkness as he listens,' or words to that effect, and then Francis says, 'The direct answer to this question is that I do of course go down into the subway, to get home, but I am still a human being, even if dismayed

and discouraged.'" The last sentence is so much in Haniel's
own tone that I can almost hear his harsh delighted laughter
in its wake.

If the tangent relationships were inevitably intense, he
and Alice each knew that he was safely centered in her
and in their marriage. They were as different as night and
day: she moved entirely from intuitive wisdom, the most
feminine being I think I have ever known, and was rooted
in him; he, hungry for knowledge, a man compelled to reach
out constantly, to experience to the full all that came his
way—books, music, landscapes, friendships—attracted people like a magnet, and then had to learn how to fend them
off. Often a visitor to their house must have wondered at
first what this intellectual being could see in what appeared
to be a retarded child; on his second visit, eating homemade
bread and butter, he might hear one of Alice's casual pro-
nouncements and find himself turn to her in surprise; and
by his third visit he could see. Women of Alice's kind are
rare in America, as unpretentious as the morning sun, as in-
genuous as the dove, as wise as the serpent.

Somehow the essence of their marriage, their amused
tolerance of each other, their imaginative concern, the quality each brought to the other, is preserved for me in two
paragraphs from letters they wrote me on the same day, when
Haniel was remaking his life around his failing eyesight.
Alice speaks first (it was October of 1950): "Our days are so
lovely, each one. Haniel brought me five roses yesterday.
They are full blown today. And just now I have picked sweet
peas in a big handful. Haniel had to go slowly last week. I
guess we had too many people the week before. We sent
away for a book on Renoir in color and it came about Friday
so we spent the weekend with him, I tell Haniel. It seems the
more effort Haniel has to see, the more he gets out of color
and landscape. He has a pair of binoculars that he hangs on

his neck when he goes for a walk, and our dog is so patient to wait while he looks."

Haniel wrote: "I am feeling a great deal better and I must tell you that even when I was not well, I was having tremendous delight in a pair of binoculars that I bought during the summer from a cousin of mine. They are wonderful glasses, and will even bring clearly into vision single trees on the mountains. As you know, my sight has been blurred for years, both for line and color, and I was quite afraid of this blurring, because the optic nerve is important to me in my writing. I had no idea the binoculars would so quickly restore it. I see one beautiful picture after another. In fact, the first time I ever raised them to my eyes, sitting in a deck chair behind the house, lo and behold, a golden bird swam into my vision and took some honey from a pentstemon. I don't know when I had seen a bird so close. You can imagine that I go around with the binoculars all the time, and I suppose I am becoming a marked figure on the Santa Fe streets. It is also quite a boon to me when I take the dog for a walk, because I can occupy myself during those interminable intervals when he stops to smell."

The dog, an old woolly terrier, who was the occasion for this lovely example of how the values within a single event may change with the angle of vision, was a beloved member of the family whose goings-out and comings-in were fervently watched and attended to.

At the end of their lives, their mutual dependence increased. Haniel depended on Alice for all reading, and she herself began to grow deaf. In February of '55 he speaks of this in a characteristic way, for, for him as for her, further limitations would release deeper powers. "Alice and I are quite close together these days. We are using a book called *The New Way to Better Hearing* to attack her hearing difficulties, which seem to be of the sort that generally come after sixty-five. The book interests me because it parallels in many ways what Dr. Bates says about eye trouble. The point in both is that nearly always damage to eye and ear leaves untouched a great residue of ability to see or to hear. This is due to the fact that it is really the brain that sees and hears and so it has to be the brain that is trained. And the brain, very simply, has to be trained to be alert. The apathy of the deaf and of so many eye cases is exactly the same as the apathy about living I feel on all sides.

"Alice, of course, blossoms when she is in a predicament. She should never have been the daughter of plenty. Difficulties, increasing her horizons, make her happy and herself. She is still the pioneer."

When Alice a year later became seriously ill, it was with the hope of gaining strength with which to nurse her that Haniel decided to undergo a serious operation on his heart at the Mayo clinic. She was in the hospital in Santa Fe; he made the journey without her. She died while he was being operated on, and he did not survive her by as much as three days. So it was right with them to the end. He had said it earlier, in a poem written after one of the operations on his eyes, "The Phoenix to the Lord" *:

> To perish, yielding all; then out of the ember
> To rise again, to yield all—and to perish:
> Never was fire so much my chrysalis,
> Nor death so much my birth.
> It was most perfect, and in every thing.
> From the first moment that the fire entwined me,
> Making me fear I lacked the courage for it,
> Until thou camest into the fire with me,
> I would not change it in the smallest way.

* From *The Grist Mill*, p. 34. This was among the poems of Haniel Long chosen and read by Witter Brynner at the joint memorial service held for Alice and Haniel Long in Santa Fe, October 21, 1956.

Let me set them once more against their landscape on an April morning, when it is Alice who makes the notation, "Today it is so refreshing to breathe and see the delicate pink of the apricot against the mist on the mountain."

—May Sarton

Marc Turian at *La Roselle*

SEVEN

Marc
The Vigneron

My friend Marc Turian is a Swiss vigneron. Most people do
not think of vineyards when they think of Switzerland; cow-
bells and clocks and chocolate, yes, but not vineyards and
the mysteries of wine. Yet wine is one of the oldest industries
of the Swiss. Legend has it that the blacksmith Helicon made
his fortune in Rome and then went back to his native land
taking olive oil, fruit, and the root of a vine that became the
Roman ancestor of all the Swiss white wines. Little by little,
the banks of the Rhone and the warm slopes of the lakes of
Neuchâtel and Léman were terraced and planted with vines.
Rain tore the earth down, and men carried it up the steep
hillsides in baskets on their backs, mended the stone terraces
every spring, hoed, fertilized, pinched back the young shoots,

and hoped for that not impossible good year that hangs over
every vineyard like a mirage.

Marc Turian's family settled three hundred years ago at
Satigny, just back of Geneva, in territory that was then
French and is still passionately Francophile. Up from the
banks of the Rhone to the stern, steep profile of the Jura
climb the vineyards, including those of La Roselle, the
Turian property. People who have held the same land over
several generations, who cut a crest in the stone portals of
their farms, the *patrons* who know the taste of their own
wine and regard vine-growing as an art rather than a trade,
might be called the aristocracy of the peasantry; of such are
the Turians.

In Marc's complex nature there is one steadfast passion
—that of the producer of a small wine who works hard to
make it better each year, even though this may be, financially speaking, a losing battle. For in the Swiss economy the
wine industry has been sacrificed, and cheap wine imported
from France, Italy, and Spain floods the market, a counter
used in the exchange of products like watches, chocolate,
electrical power, and locomotives. And, of course, the Swiss
"name" wines have never been able to compete with the
great French ones. Many a vigneron in the valley of the
Rhone has to borrow money from the bank to pay off his
grape pickers at the vintage; many a vintage just covers the
year's debts. When I first saw Marc in the late 1940s, he
was in severe financial straits; he was facing having to sell
land as the only way out. For such a man, selling land can
be compared only to selling a thumb or a hand. One can
live without a thumb, but the idea is repugnant. It is significant that over the years the village of Satigny has had
its share of "crimes of passion," but the passion was for
land; someone was roused to homicidal fury over a question

of inheritance of those ancient vineyards that hardly pay
their way.

In the fall of '56 as I drove out from Geneva and came to
the rolling plateau, brilliant green in the evening light
against the purple wall of the Jura, I wondered how much
of it was still Marc's and how much he had given up since
my last visit. I was full of these thoughts and anxieties when
we met. There he was, a great oak of a man, swelling his
bright-blue shirt as if he would burst out of it, a man in his
middle fifties with something of the look of a benign teddy
bear; a teddy bear from the front, in profile a Roman emperor—that perfectly straight nose, massive forehead and
chin; his hands, the hands of a workman, capable of great
delicacy, though black-grained and stubby. Standing there
in thick, muddy boots, he seemed the image of an earth-
bound farmer, but his first words, after we had greeted each
other, were not of the weather or of the possible harvest.
His first words were, "You know, the Duchesse de Guermantes is dead." This singular greeting was so perfectly in
character that I have been turning it over in my mind ever
since, listening to its reverberations. For, firmly rooted
though he may be on the hillside at Satigny, the world of
Marc's imagination, which constantly flows into the real one
and out again, is tethered nowhere and carries him, like
Ariel, to the far corners of the earth in the twinkling of an
eye. His inner life is so rich in fantasy that at times one feels
that he will vanish into it and never be seen again. The death
of a woman who had been a model for one of Proust's characters seemed, of all the events of the summer, the one significant one to Marc. Here, for once, the real world and the
world of imagination were perfectly blended in a news item.

When Marc, standing at the gate, said that the Duchesse
de Guermantes was dead, I knew that I was back at La

Roselle. Marc's house sits at the bottom of the hill, where
the vines leave off. Close to the village street, it is well hidden behind a high wall and iron gate, and by a linden tree.
It was once a convent, this high stone house with its over-
hanging roof, faded green shutters against distempered walls,
rough cobbled courtyard where the usual blue and pink
hydrangeas in wooden tubs stand about, and just then (for
it was late September) the foreground taken up with huge
casks and vats being cleaned and caulked for the vintage.
It is a house that over the last fifty years has been softened
and made rich by the presence of three women, and one
cannot begin to understand Marc without considering them.
For, since he lost his father when he was a baby, his character has been stamped by feminine influences, and though
he radiates masculine sunshine, his nature has a lunar aspect,
which sheds a less obvious light.

In the old days, La Roselle belonged to Marc's aunt, a
power in the village, who delighted in gossip and ferreted out
both sides of every story. Although he lived with his mother
until her death, she has always seemed a shadowy figure.
His aunt's powerful personality dominated his childhood,
and she must have felt a peculiar tenderness for him. As a
boy, Marc had trouble with one foot and had to wear a
special boot; even now, his walk is a rolling gait, rather like
that of a sea captain holding the deck in a heavy sea, but
this slightly irregular walk is so much a part of his rhythm
and personality that it does not seem like an infirmity. As a
child, however, he was set apart; when other children were
playing out-of-doors, he was more often than not sitting on
a stool at his aunt's side. There he listened as she read the
great French poets aloud; there he was plunged into wonder
as she passed him the heavy volumes of the Larousse En-
cyclopedia, one by one. Through his aunt he learned pride
in his family and race, the sense of being "somebody," and a

certain independence in relation to the village. He has always gone his own way.

When the vignerons banded together to form a cooperative, he sold his own equipment and became a founding member of what amounts to a small wine factory. But I think Marc was never entirely happy about this affair; the hope was that by pooling resources and cutting costs the society could produce wine cheap enough to compete with the mass importation of gross French and Italian wines. But at the cooperative press, of course, all the grapes are dumped in together, and the incentive to improve the vintage of one hillside or another, the complex art of the vigneron working with his own wines, is lost.

Possibly Marc was relieved when, after four years, the associates split up over a business matter. At any rate, he led the minority opposition and, with a few other vignerons, finally withdrew and went back to being the *patron* of his own cellar, responsible for growing, producing, and selling his own wine. Getting out meant investing again in a winepress, casks, and all the other machinery of the vintage, as well as hiring his own labor. It nearly ended in ruin. But he has certainly never regretted his decision. By it he won back his honor; he could open a bottle of La Roselle again, as all the Turians had done for three hundred years. He was back in the stream of his own history.

As a boy, under his aunt's influence, he had dreamed of a university education. But there was really no question of choice; his mother needed help, and when he was eighteen he took over a man's responsibilities as manager of her estate. It is just as well, perhaps, that a curiosity so childlike and various, so undogmatic and fluid, has been allowed to go its own way—that, like the wine of La Roselle, its master is not a factory product educated just like everyone else.

One branch of his grandfather's family emigrated to

Uruguay. Now and then, over the years, one or another of these transplanted cousins came back, homesick for the long sweep of hills down to the Rhone, for the French language, for Satigny the village. They came back bringing their tales of adventure and success; looking, in their Paris clothes, like strange, opulent birds; they came back to dazzle the little boy—*she* came back. For the second powerful feminine influence in Marc's life was one of these Uruguay cousins, Elizabeth, a few years older than he. She took the boy under her wing, and became the center of his emotional life for many years.

When the aunt died, and Marc, in his early thirties, inherited La Roselle, Elizabeth, at his invitation, took over the upper floor for her own, and spent months at a time at Satigny, bringing books, flowers, her beautiful presence into the cold stone house, and creating a garden at the foot of the vines. It was, no doubt, at this time that Marc began his long explorations of Proust, losing himself in dreams of that hothouse world of experience and sensation that Elizabeth symbolized for him. She had come back to Satigny first when he was still a boy and she was already—or seemed to him—a personage in her own right. She must have sensed under his peasant ways the imaginative, singular creature waiting for a magic wand to wake him. And there is no doubt that she carried the wand, became his fairy princess, and for years captivated him, so that as long as she lived, he never wished to marry.

Yet when Elizabeth's sophisticated friends came out from Geneva for a day in the country, Marc was too shy to do more than peep over the wall at the Proustian world coming to life in his own domain. This somewhat ambiguous relationship with a cousin older than he must have intensified the split between his two worlds, for although he took Elizabeth into his circle, he remained an outsider in hers. He was forced to build an inner life for himself, a life which found expression in his own room downstairs. Because this is where the secret side of his life becomes visible, Marc rarely invites anyone in. I remember vividly the first time I saw it. I remember how incongruous the huge pair of muddy boots looked on the soft elegant carpet with its design of ocean liners. (*"Fuir! là-bas fuir!"*) One whole wall is covered with books to the ceiling; the three others are filled with paintings by contemporary Swiss painters. The desk is a rich disorder of literary, agricultural, and political journals. There are always unemptied ashtrays, bearing the faint, sweet scent of his Dutch tobacco, which fills the air with a remembrance of hay and wild flowers. Open the door and you are in an artist's room, a poet's room, but hardly (you would have thought) the room of a hardworking vigneron.

With his cousin's death, La Roselle was, for the first time, without the presence of a woman; it must have seemed a desert, and Marc must have felt himself moving through a world that had lost its meaning. It was not strange that he turned a year later to a woman of Elizabeth's circle, to an artist. Happily, in Meta Budry he found a wife whose imagination, independent spirit, and flair for living matched his own. Meta and my mother were students together at the art school in Zurich forty years ago; it is through Meta that I have come to know La Roselle. Nothing about this marriage in the autumn of life is ordinary. The house is still divided horizontally into a masculine domain on the ground floor and a feminine domain above it. On the ground floor, Marc and Emilia, the Italian cook, do all the planning of meals and the cooking for the workmen as well as the family, and here also is the small, cozy dining room, which is the heart of the house. There is a comfortable old sofa in the window, a round table, an open hearth, two glowing still lifes on the wall, shelves of cookbooks in one corner, and on the top of the highboy, where Griboule chooses to eat, several cat's dishes. Here every morning at seven or before, the shutters are thrown back and the day begins; here, during the daytime, the buyers come to order a barrel of wine, which Marc will deliver in his old Chrysler when he gets around to it; here every evening the baker leaves a big round loaf of bread on the window sill; Griboule appears like a gray ghost at the window, and Marc throws a fagot—a bunch of dry vine twigs—on the open fire and then a thick vine root, which will burn half the night when he sits listening to plays and concerts over the radio from Prague, Vienna, Paris, London. This is Marc's domain.

Meta's begins halfway up the stairs, which are stone. On the landing, there is sure to be a great copper brazier of flowers. Meta is the gardener, bringing in sheaves of roses, zinnias, asters, and chrysanthemums, which she will spend the morning arranging. Upstairs there is order and grace— an elegant drawing room, soft rich colors, flowers, that small gray eminence, Griboule, rolled up in a tight ball on a fur throw on the bed. When Marc comes up each morning at about ten, he puts on felt slippers over his boots, and he looms here like some primeval god making a visitation. He has been out into the vineyards to give his orders to the workmen and lend them a hand; he has stopped to gather a plateful of ripe figs from the fig tree; he has been over to the barn across the street; and now he comes to squeeze his huge bulk into a Louis XIV armchair and have a talk with his wife. Relaxing, he fills his pipe, and the fantasies he has been brewing since seven are released in the clouds of smoke.

Conversation with Marc is an exercise in metaphor. He throws his ideas into the air like a juggler, slightly surprised himself at their shape and lightness, his eyes sparkling suddenly. For instance, once when I was there, Griboule had been on a night out, and a mouse had found its way into a drawer and eaten a hole in a silk blouse. On being informed of this domestic catastrophe, Marc was off on the wings of metaphor. "That mouse," he announced in a puff of smoke, "was an *entrechat*."

When there is a guest in the house, a third domain is opened up—a great attic room with one wall knocked out to make a long window, which opens on the sweep of vines up the hill, on the water tower, the red tiled roof of the church, and finally the cloud-capturing wall of the Jura. From here, one can hear the laughter downstairs, which means that the day has begun.

Two years ago, when I was staying at La Roselle, Marc's fantasies took the shape of pretending to wish he had a factory job; he would embroider the joy it would be to set out on a bicycle each morning and go into a quiet, clean factory, without an anxiety or responsibility to bear. Later, as his financial predicament began to get really frightening and the bailiffs were at the door, he would dream of setting out on foot, a knapsack on his back, to see all the cathedrals in France, sleeping in haystacks, a volume of Péguy in his pocket.

One morning he said, "Let's pay a visit to Voltaire; let us go to France." The rest of the morning was spent preparing an enormous picnic, and at noon we set off for France, for Ferney—only to find the gate locked. But what matter? We had spent a whole day talking about Voltaire, and we could imagine Ferney very well. From Marc's point of view, we had actually been there.

Marc does nothing quickly. He broods over every plan, taking it out, putting it back again, not to be hurried. The bailiffs were at the door, and he could not make up his mind to sell land. Instead—and this is typical—he suddenly decided, after a long period of rumination, to buy. Borrowing from the bank, using his house as security, he bought some acres in a small town that might soon become a suburb of Geneva. Such speculations require courage and patience, of course. Marc waited, though to wait meant to risk losing La Roselle. But every vigneron must have a gambler in him, and this time the gamble, though fantastic, has paid off. The danger is past. Marc no longer speaks of setting off with a knapsack on his back as a pilgrim to France, or of working in a factory for greater peace of mind.

This was, indeed, the most erratic of his fantasies, for never was a man more addicted to his own independence. I have often wanted to accompany him through one of his rich and various days. What does he do when he sets off to town with a couple of barrels of wine to deliver? One morning, I remember, he was gone for hours, and when he came back, he sauntered in bearing meringues for dessert and a little bag of candies to suck; he announced that there was a wonderful Japanese movie to be seen. But it turned out that what he had really been doing was talking the bank into another loan for another speculation, and on the strength of this he had stopped off to order a chicken for a sick friend of Meta's. This brief encounter with illness led him back to his own single and never-to-be-forgotten experience with flu. "*My* flu," he always calls it, as one might speak of "My journey to Moscow." If one has the slightest cold, Marc's memories of his flu flood back—of the great time when he lay in grandeur "upstairs" with a high fever. Was it for weeks? Was it for days? At any rate, it was fifteen years ago, in Elizabeth's time.

A part of Marc's day is spent in the kitchen; here his imagination can go happily to work. With the intransigence of the true artist, he interrupts Emilia to slide a just-invented sauce in beside her baked eggplant or spaghetti. He opens the oven door "just to take a look" when a blast of air may be fatal to a soufflé. He's always in a good humor, always tasting whatever is in the making. Occasionally, Emilia has a tantrum and throws up her hands. But no one can be angry very long with one who wears the armor of innocence.

Everything in the ordinary world of our time works against the kind of life Marc chooses to lead. He takes on the aspect of a legend for me as soon as I find myself at a distance from him, as soon as I look back, because he is like a final explosion of individuality and character under circumstances that will soon no longer exist, even in Satigny, where the big factory for pressing anonymous grapes dominates the village. I see him, in my mind's eye, walking ahead of me between the orderly rows of vines that come to his thigh, stopping to taste a grape now and then, until we reach the top of the hill and stand for a moment looking down over the valley where his parents and grandparents and great-grandparents have worked the same vineyards. His bright-blue shirt, his pure profile of a Roman emperor stand out alone in all that green landscape; he looks as if he were surveying an empire. What will the vintage be like?

Last year, on the very day of the grape picking, it snowed; the harvest was made in silence, the vintage ruined at the eleventh hour. Three years ago there was a long drought, and the grapes shriveled. In 1957 it rained buckets during July and August. There was hope if September proved sunny, for a gold September makes a golden wine, softens the tough skins of the grapes, and makes them translucent. But September hesitated and then veered toward cloudy days—a few tantalizing hours of sun, no more. Thirty thousand litres of wine lie in the long ranges of vine on that hillside, the wine of La Roselle. But while I was there, in those crucial days just before the vintage, Marc never looked at the variable sky with impatience or grew somber when it rained. Calmly he ordered a thousand kilos of sugar, cleaned

and calked the casks, and oiled the press. There was no way
of telling the quality of the vintage, and so with the patience
of an artist and the wisdom of a philosopher, he stood and
waited for the year of the wine to turn. But in the back of
his mind, you know, there was the Duchesse de Guermantes!

It was this extravagant romantic hidden in the burly
peasant, I suppose, that has kept Marc alive in my imagination and made me wish to celebrate him here among people
with whom my connection went much deeper. That—and
something else. I am drawn to people, for I am one myself,
for whom literature is a passion, deep rather than wide
readers, who discover the great works as Marc had discovered Proust, feel themselves companioned by certain
writers throughout a lifetime, follow every clue about the
invention of the characters in their books, one might almost
say lead double lives. Marc is an extreme example of such
a person, an exemplar of the ways in which an outwardly
harsh life may be drenched in poetry. So for me he himself
has become a kind of myth, one which I still ponder.

Quig's house at left of Nelson Town Hall

Quig with Mildred and their children, 1942

EIGHT

Quig
The Painter

ALBERT QUIGLEY, or "Quig"—how well his nickname suited him! Even now, I cannot say it aloud without a feeling of warmth about my heart, a gaiety of spirit, as if a delightful breeze were rising, a sense of elation. When I moved to the remote village of Nelson, New Hampshire, not far from Monadnock mountain, I was after solitude, a rooted place where I could work in peace. I knew no one in the village and, at first, was far too absorbed in rebuilding my own house and in settling in to be conscious of my neighbors. The thrill was an oriole that I saw and heard singing at the top of one of my old maples.

But as I look back on this flight into solitude, and on all that the house and the village came to mean in the fifteen years I spent there, it seems to me that the first time I saw

Quig, if I had had any prescience, I might have thought of the greeting lonely Bushmen give each other when they meet in their desert wilderness and the first one says, "Good day! I saw you from afar and I am dying of hunger." The stranger answers, "Good day! I have been dead, but now that you have come, I live again."

Quig was always hungry for companionship with someone who could understand what his life was all about. I had been through a grueling personal experience, and had come to Nelson to find my own life again, alone. We were both living on the edge of nowhere, with our backs against the wall. But the Quigs had been here in Nelson for thirty years, and I had only just arrived. It was October.

Almost at once I began to find out how much I had to learn. For at first glance the Quigley household seemed to be a general chaos; at that time Mildred Quigley was going every morning to cook for and nurse the postman's sick wife, get her up and dressed, feed her and the cats, and bring order out of that other chaos up the road, and she had little time for her own house. The trestle table Quig had made from one wide pine board might have unwashed dishes strewn about on it, but it also often had a broken violin he was mending, or parts of a picture frame he was putting together. He was also rebuilding the house itself, so there were piles of lumber lying about and one's eyes rested on an unfinished wall . . . it took a while for me to realize what richness of life all these half-finished things represented.

Meanwhile I had already begun to understand that Quig was an unhoped-for friend, at a time when I needed just the particular friend he turned out to be. At first glance he looked like a countryman, dressed often in a plaid shirt and heavy boots, a crest of white hair and thick dark eyebrows over a rugged face—these suggested an outdoor character who would enjoy hunting and fishing. Only when one came

to know him did the extreme sensitivity of the man within
his disguise come through. The eyebrows, for instance, were
mobile. Did they actually tremble sometimes like the delicate
furry antennae of a moth? As I grew to know him, I saw how
sensitive he was to atmospheres, to textures, to every shade
of color, to tones of voice, as sensitive as he was to the sound
of his violin when he tucked it under his chin to tune it, his
head cocked a little. I saw the tenderness in his dark eyes,
their shyness, the way he tried to hide (but could not) the
fact that feeling was always close to the surface. But no one
could miss the humor in this face.

Soon after I moved in, I invited the the Quigs over for
a drink. I lit a fire in the big fireplace and had put some
yellow chrysanthemums in a blue jar on the old table. I felt
that the seventeenth-century heavy Flemish furniture which
had found its way to this New England village from our old
farmhouse in Wondelgem, Belgium, suited the house. But
it was not exactly what people might expect. So I had been
a little nervous before the arrival of these, my first guests
from the village.

Mildred and I were soon launched on all sorts of talk
about their children, about Cora Tolman who had lived
there before me, about various neighbors. I noticed that
Quig, holding his drink in one hand, was silent. After some
time, he came back to us and said quite quietly, "I have been
silent because I am looking. I am so moved by this furniture
—it is so beautiful." he said, glancing over at the great bahut,
a Flemish cupboard with curved pillars built into the sides,
which shines a deep chestnut color, rather rough and rather
splendid. It was my first experience of what I liked to call
"a fit of looking" on Quig's part. He was as absorbed in what
his eyes registered at such times as a person is whose ears
are wholly absorbed in listening to music, and he had the
same abstracted expression. I don't suppose anyone ever came

into that house who felt it more, and I was very much touched.

It is hard to remember; did we dive right into intimacy that first day, so no tentative approaches were necessary? At any rate I soon knew that I could talk with Quig about my work, as one can only talk to a fellow craftsman. Our crafts were different, but we had the same difficulties in getting started, the same despair sometimes at the end of a morning's struggle when nothing had quite "come out," the same hours of sudden triumph; it was wonderful to be able to share all this. Fairly often one or the other of us crossed the green about noon and exchanged not the time of day so much as "the state of the work." No one could come close to Quig without being aware of his warmth, the belief he poured out about art itself and the value of the artist's life, the way he entered into the problem. His own life had been a perpetual war with material circumstances to find time to paint at all, yet I never heard him complain about that. He blamed himself for not doing better and—in his sixties when I came to know him—attacked each new day with the anxious eagerness of a boy.

Little by little I was able to piece together what had made him the complex human being he was.

Albert D. Quigley, to give him his full name for once, was not a New Hampshire boy. He had come from Maine and had the sea in his blood; his father was of Irish descent, but had run away to sea rather than be confirmed into the Catholic Church (and Quig inherited this dislike of established religion). The elder Quigley was a stonecutter and taught his son the trade in a village where everything was owned by the firm, including the general store. But it must have been evident early on that Quig had other talents . . . he was musical and taught himself to play the violin, helped by the old violin maker, Alec Beckler, whose portrait he later

painted and from whom he learned one of the many skills
he had in his knapsack—rebuilding broken instruments and
even making violins himself. Those years in Maine were
rich in visual images which the young man stored up; how
many of the later paintings are memories? I possess one of
smelt fishers getting ready to set up their nets, all in smoky
grays and blues, which change as the light changes in the
room so that, as a painting to live with, it is inexhaustible.
There was something large and dreamy about Quig that
suggested the sea at the back of his mind. He was not one of
the tight-lipped, reserved people of these hills. There was a
distance in his eyes.

After his father's death, when Quig was in his mid-
twenties, World War I came. He went to France in the
Signal Corps, and when he came back, he was a changed
man. He never talked in my presence about war experiences
—what he talked about was the experience of France. When
I met Quig it had been forty years since he had seen France,
but it seemed as if he remembered every village, every tree
and winding road, every plastered wall with a geranium on
top of it, as if he had seen them yesterday. This crude Maine
stonecutter in his mid-twenties was an unlikely doughboy:
not for him the search for women or cafés. When he had a
few hours or a day off he set out on foot to explore the
countryside, observing, noting with those eyes as retentive
and piercing as a hawk's. And there in France the painter
was born.

There was no GI bill in those days, but the AEF set up a
school in Bellevue and there Quig studied after he was de-
mobilized. One of my dreams was to take Mildred and Quig
back to France for a few weeks. It never did happen, but
we imagined what it would be like and often talked of it, and
the imagining was so real for all three of us that we almost
felt we had made the trip.

Of course it was out of the question for Quig when he came back from the war to think of earning a living as a painter, at least at first, and he went back to stonecutting, then photography. There in Keene, New Hampshire, he met Mildred and there his real life began, for this was a "marriage of true minds" if I ever saw one. Quig never had an easy time . . . no man with his aspirations could have an easy time. But he had in his life two pieces of extraordinary luck. The first was when, at a table in a restaurant, he saw that haunting, intense, reserved face of a young woman whose own circumstances had made her if not morose, at least wilfully determined to go it alone—come hell or high water. She was a piece of lonely bitterness, working as clerk, walking down the street (as she told me) with her hat pulled down over her eyes. It was like Quig to recognize her, when he was walking to work some days later, and like Quig to make the instinctive, natural gesture: he flipped the hat up so he could see her face. He said, "Let's go for a walk." That walk was the first of many that took them down every street in Keene to its end—sometimes miles and miles.

If ever a man needed a wife with the courage of a lion, it was Quig, and he found it in Mildred, so small that she looked as if a breeze might blow her away, so valiant that a hurricane would not budge her if she had decided to stay put. Their life was shared in its every aspect: how often I dropped in to find Mildred putting gold leaf on a frame—work Quig had begun but not gotten around to finishing. How often I found them under the circle of light of the green student lamp playing cribbage together. They were both great readers, avid for life in all its forms, lovers of children (they had three as the years went on) and of animals: there was usually a cat snoozing on the arm of a chair, and when I first knew them there was also an old spaniel called Honey.

It was not only that these two shared an arduous life, but

they had so much fun together! When Quig was feeling merry, he liked to cook up braised beef, and on special occasions open a bottle of Chianti to go with it. He also liked to make jonnycakes and muffins, which did not always come out so well as he hoped they would. They were both great storytellers, so, when one found oneself in their company, the riches poured out on each side. They were—and Mildred is—people full of lore of all sorts. And they could match wits with almost anyone on almost any subject that came up.

But one has to envision all this rich life against a continual struggle to make ends meet. When they came to Nelson, Quig took over a shiplike piece of a house and rebuilt it with his own hands. These were the depression years; Quig worked on the night shift at the Harrisville woolen mill as a tender from three to eleven at night. That meant that he could have his real life in the daytime—as a painter, as a maker of violins, as a frame maker, as a housebuilder, as a father and husband. He also embarked on a new career as fiddler for the square dances—a fashion that swept the country in the late twenties and early thirties. The Nelson Town Hall has an exceptionally good floor for dances. On weekends Quig was often away in Fitzwilliam, Keene, or even as far south as Worcester or Boston, fiddling.

During all these activities the door of the old house was never locked; there was someone dropping in for a talk at almost any time of night or day. But Quig had a haven when the mood to paint was on him—he made himself a studio in the top floor of the unused brick schoolhouse next door. There he could take refuge from all the unfinished business at home and spend a spate of hours in front of a canvas, meditating and doing what he loved most to do and what he did best of all. Talking with him I realized freshly how much like writing a poem painting can be. It too cannot be done on will. The spirit must move. But when the spirit moved, this man who often seemed to be puttering about among a thousand and one unfinished tasks came wholly into focus. Then his concentration was absolute. There was a wonderful silence up in the old schoolhouse, such a living silence that it seemed more vivid than any word. There Quig knew who he was meant to be.

The second extraordinary piece of luck was connected with the artist in Quig. It was his friendship with Alexander James, who lived in nearby Dublin—Alec, son of William James, bawdy, fresh, nervy as a racehorse, a remarkable painter of portraits who was eaten up with conflict about his work. Alec and Quig fitted into each other's needs like brothers. As I write of them I evoke the long companionly silences as they painted side by side, then the break and the laughter as they rivaled each other in telling outrageous stories. Alec, of the New England aristocracy, rich by comparison, living in a beautiful house with an immense studio made out of a barn; Quig, stonecutter's son, mill worker, exdoughboy, fiddler—their differences melted in the passion they shared for their craft and art.

For Alec, Quig was like an older brother, less volatile, sturdier, less conflicted, perhaps partly because he was not wholly committed to painting, not a professional with all the weight of reputation and competition in the market to burden him, as it did Alec. There was a wholeness and sturdiness about Quig that must often have worked as a balm. On the other hand, Alec taught Quig much about technique, about brushes, canvas, paint itself, taught him expensive tastes in these matters—and helped him to pay for these extravagant materials by using Quig as his own framer and getting him orders from other customers as well. "Dear old Quig," as Alec called him, represented perhaps the pure unadulterated person, the free man, above all the one person to whom he could talk freely about his own anxieties and problems. Like any real friendship—and this was a great one—it sprang out of mutual need and was nourished from mutual riches. And no one outside the two men will ever know the depth of it.

But without Mildred, who stayed home with the three little children, none of it would have been possible. It was her generosity and understanding that left Quig free, free to come and go into that other world, without the slightest stain of reproach on her side or of guilt on his. Even very good marriages indeed have their times of stress. It is the measure of the reality of this one that the intense "engagement" between Alec and Quig was allowed free play, without a shadow.

When I met Quig, Alec was already dead—he died too young of a heart attack—but I don't suppose I ever talked seriously with the lonely survivor of that friendship without Alec's name coming up.

I have not spoken yet of one of Quig's salient characteristics, his love of ceremony. He was not a great drinker, but what he loved, as he often told me, was the ceremony: the fire lit, the enclosed peaceful hour when he and Mildred came to sit by my fire, the flowers, the talk, framed all in the "ceremony" of a cocktail. (I am amused at the juxtaposition of two unlikely words!) We never met, we three, for an hour at the end of the arduous day, without feeling that something of moment had happened between us; we never talked without the talk turning on "real things"—relationship and all its mysteries, art and all its mysteries, nature and all its mysteries.

For me, to be with the Quigs was in some deep sense to come *home*: come home to the values with which I had grown up, and which so often appeared to be anachronistic in life as it is lived in the United States. For one thing, the world we shared, in "ceremony," was completely uncompetitive. Status—social, professional—had no place here. We found ourselves conversing like three philosophers about the things that *really* matter. When I bought my house in Nelson, I had imagined solitude and peace, but I had not imagined this being restored to the values with which I had grown up, and which after the death of my scholar-father and my artist-mother I had begun to believe could be found only in Europe.

Ceremony, laughter, tenderness . . . Quig had them all in large measure, and all are exemplified in a story he told me about the time he was working in the mill. Among his fellow workers at that time was an old man who had periodic heart attacks, as everyone was aware. This old man remembered the folk dances of Nova Scotia and asked Quig if he would not bring his violin and play some of the old tunes at their lunch break. So one day they went down to the cellar with their sandwiches and coffee, and Quig played the jigs and reels buried deep in the old man's memory. So spirited was the playing and so spirited the memory, that the listener was moved to get up and dance; dance he did, old and sick as he was, in a delightful fling of restored youth. They parted to go back to work by different stairways. Later that day Quig heard that the old man had dropped dead on his way up.

But as he told it, Quig was well aware that if one had to die, as we all do, going out dancing is perhaps as good a way as any other. Was I imagining the tears that shone in Quig's eyes as he told this story? And did I tell him that it reminded me for some reason of Yeats? Yeats would have seen the point.

Quig did not "go out" fiddling, as perhaps he would have liked to do. He was much too busy building a big addition onto the house all that last year to know really that he was ill. He thought he was just tired. Single-handedly he added a new dimension to the living room and built on second-floor bedrooms above it. I am glad I lent him my new saw; maybe it helped. By late fall he had to admit that he was ill, and took to his bed. There he lay in the big room downstairs, a cat and a fiddle on the end of it; there he lay receiving callers with shy jokes about his condition, making a "ceremony" even of this last illness.

I saw him once more in a "fit of looking"—in the hospital before he died. I took him a pocket edition of Delacroix's Journal and he happened to open it to the stunning portrait of Chopin. While Mildred and I talked softly at the bedside, Quig disappeared into his world of joy, the world of the painter. I don't believe he heard a word we said, but I saw once more that concentrated light in his eyes, and he did not let the book go out of his hands while I was there.

Beside this I want to place another day, when he was well and himself. He had been working for weeks to make his first violin: delicate, absorbing, tense work. He had often mended broken instruments (people got to know that he could make something of what looked like a total wreck and brought him their broken violins as if broken human bones to a surgeon), but he had never embarked on the different adventure of starting from scratch. I happened to walk over at the end of a morning and heard the sound of a violin before I opened the door. Could it be? It was the birth of his new violin; he had lifted it to his chin and drawn a bow across the strings for the first time! For me it was a great moment to hear it sing, to hear it being given the breath of life.

Lives are framed by death. Quig had been so much a part of this landscape that perhaps we had come to take him for granted like some old tree which would surely outlive us all, its strong roots twined around granite. Then, quite suddenly, he was gone. People who had not expected to felt sharp loss—what? Quig not there? But he had always been there, always responsive, always caring. He just couldn't be dead! All sorts of people felt bereaved as if they had lost a parent, a brother, the best of friends. Somehow in the last months when he must have been feeling very ill, Quig had managed to paint the three boys of the undertaker in Keene: rare indeed is the man whose death brings tears to the eyes of the undertaker! But this man mourned, as did the village idiot to whom Quig had been kind, as did a rich woman to whom he had taught all he could about painting, as did the poet across the green (myself), as did his fellow workers at the mill—and many, many others. How many we knew when the funeral unexpectedly drew a host of people, people the family hardly knew, people from far away, people whose lives Quig's had touched and touched deeply. Only Alec was not there.

Death frames. What was framed for us on that final day is hard to put into words. All the bits and pieces of a life which often seemed scattered among too many gifts suddenly came together, and we saw him whole. The wholeness was in the tenderness toward life itself, the power of joy, the liveliness of mind, the something like triumph of a man who had tasted no worldly success but had never ceased to create and to give. I sat down that morning and wrote what I felt, wrote it quickly, almost as one makes a death mask, to catch the total being before the winds disperse it.

How rarely as a poet does one feel useful and needed! But I have never felt so proud to be published anywhere as I was when the *Keene Sentinel* published my celebration of Quig on its editorial page, and when the minister (the same man who had come to bury Alexander James) read it at the funeral itself.

Lately, he lay downstairs, a dying king,
His violin at the end of the bed like a couchant beast
In some old tapestry or heraldic painting,
The battered orange cat blinking by the fire,
The fat asthmatic dog snoring beside him—
Family, neighbors gathered there all day:

He kept his wit intact, though flesh had nearly left him.
And still he sparkled like a frost-touched leaf,
So withered now a breath might take him,
Accepting laughter as a final homage.

Before we could get used to the idea of death,
He had gone,
Before we could get used to it,
Had slipped away in the night,
Leaving this empty bag of a world—no Quig in it.
God, it's a lonely village now without him!
(Still beautiful in the snow and cruel cold—
Nelson, he animated with his warming presence.)

He was everyone's father, graced in the giving,
Prodigal of tenderness real fathers rarely give,
Enfolded us, believed, could weep like a woman,
Yet held fast to those values that stand up to death,
Kingly in this. Yet always a poor man, bills piling up,
Never out of the woods, never quite in the clear—
His last act to paint the portraits of four boys.
Somehow he did it, summoned himself, and kept his promise.

Improvident, generous, his white hair in a crest
Said, "I'm cock of the world because I love it"—
Cock, not by possession, but by love.
Maker of violins, he held them in his hands
Because he wanted the true sound, the singing tone;
Painter of this landscape and of all our faces:
We have to see now and we have to try to hear
Without his accurate, intimate eye and ear.

(Remember how he loved the early spring, its redness,
Its feathery graces, remember how he loved Cézanne,
Renoir, Degas, in those last days held in his hands
A portrait by Delacroix, and would not be distracted:
Often I have seen him silenced by a fit of looking.)

Lover of ceremony, and all courteous graces,
He was one of the last fiddlers, jigs and reels,
And "swing your partners!" We'll dance in the old hall
A last dance for Quig, the fiddler, whose tunes kept
Our feet light, our eyes open, our hearts true.
I tell you his joys are with us. We are not alone.
(But, God, it's an empty village that we have to fill!)

Part IV

—Marjorie Wells

S. S. Koteliansky with Marjorie Wells' granddaughter

NINE

S. S. Koteliansky

No ONE WHO knew him can bear to think of the house at 5 Acacia Road in St. John's Wood in London, empty. For so many years we who loved him have run the last few yards to the high green gate, pushed it open, and stopped just inside to wait for Kot, framed in the kitchen window, to lift his head from a book and wave a welcome. For so many years we have forgotten to close the gate in our pleasure at having arrived.

There he was, as certain as spring, sitting in his kitchen, the little stove blazing away at his back, the rows of plates shining on the dresser to his right, and a straight chair placed opposite him across the scrubbed deal table, waiting. This kitchen was a hearth in the most ancient sense of the word, and Kot regarded it as such. Not the slightest disorder could be permitted. The extreme plainness of the furniture, the tomatoes in a bowl on the dresser, the loaf of bread, spoke of peace and joy, as alive as they might be if Cézanne had painted them:

> "And whether He exist at all,
> The Father and the Prodigal,
> He is expected by these things
> And each plate Hosannah sings."

We came from the world to a place that was not quite the world, and sat down gratefully in this small haven of friendship. It was always a homecoming.

D. H. Lawrence called him "The Lion of Judah," or, when they were in a state of war, simply "Jehovah"; but that was long ago in the golden age before World War I, when S. S. Koteliansky, a Russian Jew from a small village in the Ukraine, arrived in England like an Old Testament prophet. Leonard Woolf said, "If you knew Kot well, you understood what a major Hebrew prophet must have been like. If Jeremiah had been born in a ghetto village of the Ukraine in 1882, he would have been Kot." Police surveillance, the fear of pogroms, had burned into this young man a character like steel, "purified of all spiritual grit," a fierce belief in the dignity of man. He was a Jew in the proudest possible way, breathing fire and brimstone against all Philistines and "blighters," as he called politicians, publishers, bad writers, and any Jew who did not come up to his high standards: "I am myself again and curse the blighters," he would say, a fierce joy in his intense black eyes. He was intransigence personified, could say no with an absolute disregard of the amenities or his own self-interest. When a mutual friend of the Lawrences telephoned him after twenty years' absence and asked whether she could come to call, Kot said simply, "No." For in the interval she had written a book about

Lawrence of which he disapproved; in vain she pleaded that after all they were old friends, that she needed to see him. Kot simply repeated, "No." It was final. But if he said yes, it was yes forever and ever, world without end.

In a time of disturbingly shifting values, Kot's remained restfully black and white. "In the hierarchy of creation there is God Almighty and Leo Tolstoy"; among the people of the earth only the English were worthy of unqualified admiration; his friends D. H. Lawrence, Katherine Mansfield, the painter Mark Gertler, and James Stephens were archangels and it did not matter what their faults may have been, nothing could alter this fact; "the Wolves," Leonard and Virginia, and the Julian Huxleys were ranged with the seraphim. A few others managed to get just inside the pale, and everyone else was somewhere in outer darkness.

If heaven is any good at all, it will be for Kot an exact replica of the house at 5 Acacia Road where Katherine Mansfield once lived—her study was on the top floor at the back, and looked out on the pear tree celebrated in "Bliss." This house was his home for thirty-eight years, from 1917 until his death; at the end of his life he hardly left it. Although he was often short of money, and should have kept the two top floors rented, this was difficult to do, as he was apt to take a dislike to any prospective lodger: "Had a fight last week. A hard-faced woman wanted to take the rooms. Through sheer inspiration I said I wanted twelve or fifteen pounds a week, so I shall never see Hard-face again. Salutations to all the young, open faces and to all those who are kind and gentle."

The four rooms where Kot lived contained, as I have suggested, a minimum of furniture, and this of the plainest. There was no "easy" chair, for instance; there were not many books, but these, the essential, notably all the Russian classics. It was kept so immaculate by Kot himself, with the help of a weekly char, that every floor shone and a speck of dust would have been sacrilege. Upstairs in the front room there was a painting by his old friend Beatrice Campbell of Kot and Katherine Mansfield sitting in deck chairs in the garden; there was a table with books and papers on it, a jar of pencils, and a little blue-green bowl given to him by K.M.; there were two or three straight chairs, a radio, and a bookcase. Here Kot often sat in the evening watching the light fade and listening to the news. He slept in the monastic back room. Belowstairs there was a dining room, never used, opening through French doors into the garden, of which he was proud because, although he himself did little work there, each plant and flower had been put in by a friend and so had become an extension of the lares and penates inside. But the center of his life was the warm, sunny kitchen, which he reached each day like an island, after making his bed, having breakfast, and washing the dishes at a dark sink down the hall. Here in the kitchen he could busy himself with the real things—books and friends.

When I knew him, he was not eager to meet new faces, but fortunately he had read my first novel in manuscript and was largely responsible for its publication by the Cresset Press, for whom he was an adviser. He told the Huxleys that I had some glimmerings of talent and so they invited us to tea together. In the midst of all the excitements of those two English springs, when I was just discovering myself as a young woman, and just opening my wings as a beginning writer, Kot appeared like warm fresh bread after almost too much champagne. He made great demands on his friends, but they were always demands in depth, demands that one be authentic. In his presence, emotions, ideas, fell suddenly into place; self-intoxication became self-searching. There was to be no nonsense, only "the truth"; and therefore a visit to him was something of an ordeal.

It was also a ceremony, planned by postcard or letter well

in advance, and eagerly awaited on both sides. It was wise to be early rather than late, or he might become impatient and "the Christian have to fight terribly hard to suppress and expel the pagan." Even when one was, as I tried to be, exactly on time, impatience sometimes made him irritable. He had been expectant for hours, or so he made one feel.

Kot's eyes, behind horn-rimmed glasses, snapped with eagerness; his wiry gray hair stood up two inches straight in the air like the élan vital itself. He looked astonished and fiercely expectant. When he laughed, his whole face broke up into laughter, and enjoyment seemed to shoot out of him in showers of sparks. In every way and about everything he did—reading a manuscript, washing sheets, building a fire— he was the opposite of superficial; he did everything with his whole being, and this meant of course that he used up an immense amount of energy and emotion in just the ordinary business of living. The rituals upon which he insisted, the definite rhythm of each day, were no doubt necessary as a balance.

So every detail had been foreseen hours before a visit. There on the table lay his box of Russian cigarettes, two cups and saucers, a jar of jam, and a tin box of thin English biscuits. Kot smoked incessantly, drank tea, ate nothing, and insisted that enormous quantities of jam and biscuits be consumed by the guest. Before World War II, when James Stephens and I were sometimes invited together, he prepared a martini of his own invention (mysterious herbs were added to the usual ingredients). After two or three helpings of this Koteliansky drink poured from a square cut-glass bottle, James would shut his eyes and rock back and forth as he recited poems in that unforgettable light, crooning voice, while Kot sat and beamed. There was less anger and more joy when James drew his magic circle around us. And Kot, for all his insistence on the "plain truth," admitted in James the

wildest fantasies and egged him on to embroider every tale
to the limit. He also demanded that his friends respect each
other, and often asked me to read a poem of mine for James's
comment, or wrote to tell me that James approved of this or
that line.

If the tea itself followed a ritual, so did the conversation.
When I saw him alone—and he preferred to see his friends
alone—Kot always began, "Well, May . . ." leaving a silence
in the air while he turned to light a long paper spill from the
coals in the stove-grate behind him, and then his cigarette.
This was an invitation to tell all that had taken place in the
last days—where you had been, whom you had seen, and
above all to give a detailed account of all meals. Kot, ascetic
himself, loved descriptions of food. This was a safe beginning.
For almost everyone turned out to be beyond the pale. "There
are pigs and people," one would be informed, "and so-and-so
is and always has been a pig." Argument was useless. Kot's
mind had been made up, it appeared, before you were born.
Rarely, very rarely he gave the accolade, "Yes, so-and-so is
a real person." That was very high praise indeed. His literary
judgments too were implacable. For he was one of the rare
readers who look upon the writing of literature as sacred
work, and the betrayal of it by shoddiness, impatience, or
simple lack of talent, an actual crime.

The acceptance of a writer by Kot was an act of faith.
Like any true believer he would then brook no criticism of
someone like Lawrence or Katherine Mansfield whom he
had accepted, although during their lifetime he himself had
criticized and badgered and given no quarter. He had, in fact,
elected himself a despotic conscience for his writer friends,
and the name "Jehovah" had been given after considerable
suffering. One did not write to Kot as to other friends; one
wrote to one's conscience, and this becomes quite clear when
I look back, for instance, at the letters Katherine Mansfield

did write to him, as in November of 1921, "I am glad you criticized me. It is right that you should have hated much in me. I was false in many things and *careless*—untrue in many ways. But I would like you to know that I recognize this and for a long time I have been trying to 'squeeze the slave out of my soul.'"

He had an unerring eye for the fake, the false note, the "literary," and would have none of it. But he had also an unerring eye for the significant, for the lasting, for the true. Twenty-five years ago he was saying that Faulkner was the one original American talent of the time. And in our last conversation, shortly before his death, he spoke with feeling of Alfred North Whitehead and Whitehead's reasons for allowing Lucian Price to record certain conversations. Kot was certain that Whitehead had done this because he had some things to say to and about America that must be said before he died. Kot often told me that in order to understand what was happening in Russia, it was necessary to read Dostoevski's *The Possessed*.

He read a great deal, but alway very slowly and very carefully, so that a new writer in his firmament would be studied for weeks and months. If he had made a real discovery he hoarded it and allowed himself only a page or so a day. During the bombing of London it was Traherne: "Traherne's simplicity and truthfulness are just amazing." Later on it was Bunyan, "Have you ever read Bunyan's *Pilgrim's Progress*? It is the most amazing literary achievement. I have been reading it for weeks during the winter. It is Bunyan who has fashioned England into what it is now, while present-day intellectuals are no more than well-paid errand boys, chattering about 'ideas.'"

He was as perspicacious about literature as he was innocent and disarmed before life. He lived each day with great intensity, as if it were the first and last day, and he was sensitive to season and weather as are all people who live alone, for whom the weather is a companion. "It is autumn here. The sun appeared on Sunday and it was beautiful; the gentle, quiet, unostentatious beauty that is England." In the autumn Kot withdrew indoors like a hibernating English animal, but in spring he became a Russian again. It was marvelous to hear him tell of spring in Russia, of how, after the dark and terrible cold, suddenly the air was full of the scent of violets and people literally went mad with joy.

The Russian in Kot was never very deeply submerged. Just under the thin English surface, the Russian suffered and rejoiced and led his natural passionate life. The crocuses in the garden reminded him of the candles in the synagogues. When he spoke the word *Kiev* (where he had studied as a young man) hundreds of churches seemed to rise up behind his eyes, suddenly very bright, and one heard the sound of bells. Kot was not orthodox, but like many "unbelievers," he was a deeply religious person, so much so that he felt it sacrilege to profane a church or a cathedral by entering it as a mere tourist. Only once he was persuaded by Lady Ottoline Morrell to attend a service in St. George's chapel at Windsor, and on this occasion was amazed and delighted to discover that the service seemed very much like an orthodox Jewish one.

Sometimes the Russian Kot was startling, as we found during the years when he had some extraordinary neighbors, known always as "the mad ones." They were a Dostoevskian group, never very clearly defined, of whom one was definitely subhuman and the others clearly not sane. I suppose that Kot learned to bear this rather horrifying propinquity by, as it were, including them in his universe, for he actually related their antics with considerable zest, their occasional violent sorties and the terrible noises they made. 5 Acacia Road is one half of a double house, and the walls were thin, so that any sound next door was audible. "With the new year, the mad ones at No. 4 have taken a new lease on life, and are screaming day and night. This is a sign of warm weather arriving." In fact when at last 4 Acacia Road was silent and empty again, there was a sense of absence, of something missing. As Kot expressed it, "At any time I prefer mad ones to sane, normal human beings." They, at least, were not "blighters."

Under his fierce mannerisms, Kot was, of course, an ultra-sensitive, so much so that during the war he disliked getting food parcels because "I don't want my friendly relations with the postman tinged with a certain envy. My postman knows the contents of every food parcel without opening it." It did not occur to Kot that this was no feat of divination since one had to write out a list of contents on a tag attached to each parcel. But small mystifications were always dear to him; and I sometimes thought that "the mad ones" were in this category of mystery and magic, which explained their fascination.

It must be clear that Kot was unadapted to life as it is lived in the world by most of us. I learned with some surprise from Leonard Woolf's obituary for him in the *New Statesman* that his father had been a prosperous millowner. Absolute purity and intransigence such as his certainly make earning a living a problem. When I knew him he was an adviser to and reader for Dennis Cohen at the Cresset Press. In the old days he had collaborated with Lawrence, Katherine Mansfield, and both "Wolves" in making translations of books by Tolstoy, Dostoevski, Tchekhov, Gorki, and Bunin; these are still among the most accurate and colloquial one can find. Leonard Woolf says, "You only learned to the full Kot's intensity and integrity by collaborating with him in a Russian translation." His English was personal and vivid, but he had a real sense of English style, and was an excellent critic. Still, all these jobs were hardly sufficient to keep a man alive. I presume that he had some small capital which must have dwindled frighteningly as the pound fell, and the cost of living rose. Now and then he sold a few first editions to collectors.

He cheered himself up by inventing fantastic schemes for "making a fortune." Hopes rose and fell each year when the results of the Irish Sweep came out: "If I win the Irish Sweep, I shall be your publisher and there will be no need to deal with the blighters." There was always the possibility that some rich American library would offer thousands of pounds for the Mansfield and Lawrence letters still in his possession. And if all else failed, there was, floating in the magic bottle of martinis, a scheme by which Kot, James Stephens, and I would live at the zoo in a comfortable cage with all food and drink provided free. "If you and James are in a cage with me, I shall no longer need or want anything. And the end of my days will be passed in happiness, serene and complete." This dream collapsed, of course, when our friend Julian Huxley left the London Zoo, of which he had been Secretary, for we could hardly accept a cage from a total stranger.

For Kot, true friends "happened like great and rare events," and on these events he staked his life. It was not only that he had imaginative genius for understanding people's inner directions, so that he could become a conscience for them; it was not only that he could give to friendship the passionate attention which only the unmarried, perhaps, have time and energy to give; it was not only that he was that terrible and lovable "Jehovah." In a world where everything was becoming more and more muddy and confused, his anger was purifying, his intransigence seemed an ancient kind of sanity just because it was so ruthless.

At the time I met Kot, at a tea at the Julian Huxleys', in their apartment over the zoo, I was just coming out into my real life, writing my first novel, with only a first book of poems behind me. "Coming out" is the exact truth about my state, for I had suddenly found out at twenty-five that I was an attractive young woman. During the years of struggle in the theatre there had been no time for dancing, for parties, for "meeting people," for fabulous encounters with the great, and all that was suddenly happening to me in 1937, in London, and went on in a great burst, a sudden flowering in every personal direction until the war three years later. I was in love with everyone and almost everyone was a little in love with me. I suppose it was a kind of delayed adolescence.

The problem, of course, was to keep my balance, and to come through a lot of false intoxications to the values by which I would live the rest of my life. I wonder whether that would have been possible without Kot's attentive and fiercely demanding friendship. Perhaps the most important thing was that he believed that I would become a good writer, and from him that meant everything, for he had an unerring eye for the authentic in literature. That strong faith built the foundation; without it I could not have stood up, perhaps, to his criticisms and doubts about me as a person. For I was, and I knew it, in many ways what my father used to call "an unlicked cub." Kot, rather like a bear himself, could lick quite furiously at times, but criticism that comes out of love is always usable and nourishing. He said in a letter, "I am so very fond of you that I should like to protect you against the ills of life. So think of it seriously, and may my wish be a shield against all ill, and a strength to you." And so it was.

He was delighted to hear that I had been invited to see Virginia Woolf several times: "When Virginia is at peace, her face is lit up by great beauty. You will have achieved very much by gaining her friendship." (It was entirely characteristic that he should speak of friendship as an achieve-

ment.) But he was disturbed, and rightly, by the multiplicity
of my *amitiés amoureuses*: "You see, I am very fond of you
and should like you to possess all virtues without a spot or
stain. You have millions of virtues, but you postpone their
practice. Hence my preaching at you. But as you are not only
a darling, but a terribly wise being, you must listen to me
seriously, although you are allowed to smile. (See what an
inconsistent person I am: for the sake of your smile, I spoil
my whole case.)" And in another letter, "I want you to be
aware of what you call your 'steel' and what I call your
wisdom, all the time. I mean that whatever mad or chaotic
things you do, never forget that there is your ultimate wisdom that must keep you safe and whole—of course I shall
be scolding you and be terribly severe, and all of this out of
very good and so tender love for you."

He did scold me sometimes, but he also understood everything because he was a passionate being and also a mystic.
"You are right. Although made of corruptible flesh, the flesh
can become spirit. And with a few it is so, and it is realized, if
not consciously, then unconsciously, very early in life. I never
doubted your flesh is spirit. Hence my belief in what you
call 'steel' and I call wisdom."

Kot's purity, his refusal to compromise in any way, made
him an invaluable friend, but these very qualities were costly
to himself of course, for in the last years they helped to iso-
late him and narrowed a life which had been magnificent in
its fundamental grasp of human affairs. Too often his response became rage toward things he could not control, and
with rage came its usual companion, depression. Once at
least he tried to commit suicide and was given shock treat-
ment which did have at least a temporary good effect. He
suffered a thrombosis after World War II and had to be hospitalized. His reaction was typical: "If Juliette tells you that
I don't obey the doctors, it is perfectly true: it is good for me

not to obey doctors. To obey I must love a person, and how could one love a doctor? Preposterous!" When at last I was able to come over to England in 1944 I found him physically much diminished, suddenly thinner and so frail it was a shock. But he could still laugh, and he spun out a marvelous tale of how he had (when he was in the hospital) one day decided that enough was enough and simply walked out in his pajamas and gone home! Kot who had given so much to his friends all his life was surrounded by loving friends in the last years. Marjorie Wells went to see him nearly every day, and Juliette Huxley as often as possible. But no one could really help the awful depressions.

I think he was often homesick for Russia, though at least World War II had brought his Canadian cousins into his orbit—they wrote to him and sent food parcels. But, one by one, he had seen fall away the friendships rooted in his life and around whom his life was rooted. After World War I, when both Katherine Mansfield and Lawrence died, nothing was ever quite the same again. Then, during and after World War II, when first Virginia Woolf, then Lady Ottoline Morrell, and finally James Stephens were taken from him, Kot felt that the world—the only world he cared about—was coming to an end. Of the pre-1914 friends only Beatrice Campbell was still there, to come over for periodic reviving visits from Ireland, and Leonard Woolf, who did come for a long talk shortly before the end, and wrote me that he feared he might have hastened it because the talk about K.M. and Lawrence had been so passionate. (But if so, that is how Kot would surely have wished to die—talking about and remembering those two whom he had loved most.)

In his obituary in the *New Statesman* that winter of '55 Leonard Woolf wrote, "There are some Jews who, though their ancestors have for centuries lived in European ghettos, are born with certain characteristics which the sun and sand

of the desert beat into the bodies and minds of Semites. The
heat of the desert burns their bodies until they are tempered
into steel; it tempers their minds until they seem to be
purified of all spiritual grit, leaving in mind and soul only
pure, undiluted, austere, fanatical passion. I am not saying
whether this is good or bad—I don't know—but aesthetically
it is austerely beautiful—in daily life it is also extremely uncomfortable."

That is true, and once or twice I experienced Kot's mania
for cleanliness and spotlessness—once when I spent two
nights there and spilled powder on a table. That was clearly
a mortal sin! But as I think back to the warm tiny kitchen
where we talked so often and so long, I realize that there is
no room in the world where I have ever felt so absolutely at
home if being at home means being comfortable spiritually,
being able to be completely myself without fear or embar-
rassment because I was sitting opposite an old man who was
completely himself and who was not afraid of a rather high
emotional temperature—in fact, thrived on it. If there is a
heaven, it looks exactly like 5 Acacia Road. Lawrence is putting a duck in the oven; K.M. is writing at her table in the
upper room; James is drinking gin and crooning poems in
the kitchen; and down at the end of the garden the pear tree
is in flower.

—Alfred Knopf

Elizabeth Bowen

TEN

Elizabeth Bowen

It was June 1936 in London, a spring when, after the disaster of my theatre, I was struggling to find my feet again, writing poems, and falling quite by chance into a great deal of life that I had neither earned nor was prepared to meet, for at twenty-four I was almost incredibly inexperienced, unworldly, and, regarding most things everyone is supposed to know after puberty, ignorant. For instance, I fell quite by chance into a cooperative house on Taviton Street to sublet a temporarily vacant room and found myself part of a group of professional men and women, among them John Summerson, whose room was next door to mine. We communicated intensely through a wall as I wrote at my desk while he played Bach on the harpsichord. At four we often shared a cup of tea, and one day he asked me whether I would like to meet Elizabeth Bowen. We were invited to dinner, he said. I felt overwhelmed with delight, but also terrified. What to wear? I did have a bright-blue taffeta evening coat that might conceal or even lift to the proper level a nondescript silk print. And a week later we were on our way in a taxi to 5 Clarence Terrace in Regent's Park. The Nash terraces are one of the beauties of London, and John was writing a book about Nash and perhaps spoke of this. I had never heard of Nash and could make no intelligent response as I stood trembling before the pillared doorway.

5 Clarence Terrace is not a very large or grand house but the drawing room on the second floor has great charm. A corner room, its long French windows on two sides were open that June night to shifting patterns of leaves illuminated by street lamps. There I was introduced to my hosts, Alan and Elizabeth Bowen Cameron, and to Isaiah Berlin (about whom I knew nothing) and David Cecil, whose biography of Cowper, *The Stricken Deer*, I had read. As dazzled as a moth by so much light, I looked around me at a bowl of white peonies reflected in the mirror over the mantel, at the huge stiff Regency sofa where Elizabeth Bowen sat, and tried to understand the precipitous flow of language, punctuated by laughter, all around me. It was a good example of culture shock as I floundered, paralyzed, in the abyss between American and Oxford English, and wondered whether I would ever catch even one word. Luckily Alan intervened to offer me a cocktail—I could understand him, and gradually I began to relax and to listen.

Alan struck me as not at all the man I might have imagined as Elizabeth's husband. He was quite stout, had a rather Blimpish look, a red face and walrus mustache, and spoke in a high voice, near falsetto. But it was clear almost at once that he was extremely kind and sensitive, and it was he who went out of his way to put me at ease.

I no longer remember what was said that evening, but what I do remember vividly was the lightness and gaiety, the laughter, the tremendous enjoyment these people obviously found in each other's company, the brilliance of it all. John and I had found it difficult to converse; mostly I had been tongue-tied in his presence, and now I knew why. Perhaps he had wanted to introduce me to Elizabeth, so that I could learn what his true element was; for I could see that this was his element, an element where learning and wit could come into play. But it was not, of course, my element, and never would be.

Little by little I found the courage to observe Elizabeth Bowen. She looked, I thought, like a drawing by Holbein. Hers was a handsome face, handsome rather than beautiful, with its bold nose, high cheekbones, and tall forehead; but the coloring was as delicate as the structure was strong— fine red-gold hair pulled straight back into a loose knot at her neck, faint eyebrows over pale-blue eyes. I was struck by her hands, which she used a great deal, often holding one in the air before her with a cigarette in it. They were awkwardly large; the heavy bracelets she wore became them. But the slight stammer and her delightful rippling laughter, rather like a purr, made her human and approachable. And she was very good at drawing a guest out; so I soon felt at ease and gloriously happy to find myself in such company.

The evening ended by her asking me suddenly, just as we were saying good-bye, to go with her to the third floor to see whether she had a copy of *To the North* left to give me. It was, she said, her favorite among her novels. She did find one and inscribed it for me. Then, guessing that my dream was to meet Virginia Woolf, she promised to try to get her and Leonard for dinner. How very kind she was to this American girl who had really nothing to offer except admiration!

Elizabeth and I did not become friends until the following spring. Conrad and Mary Aiken had offered me for three months for a small rent their house, Jeakes House, on Mermaid Street in Rye, just a few doors down from Henry James's Lamb House, looking out over the sheep-dotted salt marshes. I couldn't swing it alone, of course, but I persuaded Kappo Phelan, who had been a director in my Apprentice Theatre, and Margaret English, one of the company, and a young woman who had just graduated from Bennington to share the house and the expenses. Until then I had lived only in rented rooms in London. It was a great adventure to be on our own, responsible for housekeeping (we took turns as cooks), and to be able to invite our friends to stay on weekends. I was overjoyed when Elizabeth accepted an invitation. It's quite a long journey down from London by train and it seemed marvelous that she was willing to make it.

Something knots a friendship, or raises the emotional content to a new plane. Some final door must open between two people if they are to become true friends; a total acceptance each of the other has to take place. At twenty-five, just coming into the sense that I could be attractive, intoxicated by the worlds of love and friendship opening on every side, I fell in love every day, or so it seems as I look back, a little shocked now by the proliferation. I was lifted up on a stream of major encounters—I was seeing the Julian Huxleys often, and Koteliansky—and on a stream, too, of poetry. Elizabeth had the immense glamor (there is no greater) of being a writer I admired, and the warmth and style as a human being that made me long to be "taken in" to her life as more than a casual acquaintance. Perhaps we were a little alike in a talent for instant intimacy.

Here it may be to the point to compare her with Virginia Woolf, with whom I had had tea several times by then. One felt with Virginia Woolf (at least as a double take some hours after each encounter) that one had been in the presence of a highly sensitive, immensely curious *voyeur*, of a person who lived vicariously with the intensity that most of us live our own lives. She drew out confidences with magnetic attentiveness as she listened to the answers to her percipient questions. But she did not give. Of course her attention was flattering and every young person is delighted to be forced to analyze himself in such a presence. She had a fantastic sense of humor—fantastic in the sense that its essence was exaggeration—but she was never warm. One never felt "taken in" to her life, or even completely and unreservedly taken in to the moment, as she was experiencing it.

Elizabeth entered into the moment with the whole of herself. She had a genius for participating caringly in whatever was going on around her, and in doing so gave herself away with such generosity and openness that it could be "unnerving," to use her own word. She was truly kind . . . and she was not British. The Irish and even the Anglo-Irish, who have become over the centuries more Irish than the Irish themselves are willing to concede, glory in talking about their private lives. Elizabeth had immense dignity and reserve; yet on those late nights when I stayed at Clarence Terrace (it was impossible to get to London from Rye and back in a day) and, after the guests had gone, she fetched a pillow from her bedroom and stretched out on the sofa to smoke a last cigarette, she did tell me a great deal about herself, often in response to my endless queries and anxieties about my own life. For how can one help the young except by sharing one's own experience?

I understood that earlier in her life she had loved at least one woman, but I gathered that that period was over. Now her love affairs were with men. She seemed to take it quite naturally that she could be in love and still very much married to Alan. I was at that time bursting out of a puritan envelope, and all this amazed, touched, shook, and filled me with love for this extraordinary woman who could be at the same time so open and so grand, so much a genius and so human, and, above all, as vulnerable as I was, apparently, to sudden irrational attachments. Yet I knew that she was light-years beyond me in wisdom and in experience, that her personality was at one with itself, solid, if you will, in a way that mine was far from being. All these observations and feelings found their way into poems, none of them very good. But I think it is worth setting one down here because it still seems to me accurate.

PORTRAIT BY HOLBEIN

In a moment exaggeration,
the brilliant image
exploding in the mind
will fade like fireworks,
leaving it dark.
But for this moment
Your face is there,
landscape by lightning:
Your face is drawn in pencil,
startling the sense
with its perfected shape,
the tension of the outline,
the curious created purity—
used as a painter would, yourself,
interpreted and mastered—
the comment of the mind.

It took me years to understand that the poem one writes out of love and brings to its subject as a present is not always as delightful to receive as it is to give. For poems of this kind are always pleas and must, often, be warded off out of kindness. It was one of Elizabeth's graces that she could accept them quite simply as gifts, and allow herself, momentarily, to be carried on their stream.

There was a full moon on the night she spent at Jeakes House in late May. My study, high up, with a large studio window, looked out over the roofs and chimney pots to the wide lonely marshes, misty in the moonlight. We sat there, talking, sometimes silent, for a long hour after dinner, and finally Elizabeth, so sensitized to atmosphere, to place, to the total content of a moment, responded to my passionate feelings for her. We slept together in my big bed after an exchange that had great tenderness in it.

For me it was the climax of weeks of growing intensity. But, as I see it now, I understand perfectly what it was for Elizabeth—a moment of beauty, of release from tension, when she was in a state herself of emotional precipitation that had nothing to do with me. She was on her way to Boulogne to meet a man who was to become her lover. And a few days later I had a very kind, dear letter from her, telling me the truth. For me that romantic night meant not the beginning of a love affair, but the seal set on a friendship.

But what was I to do with all this feeling? Instead of living it out, or perhaps I should say the only way I could live it out, was to write a novel. In my first novel Elizabeth appears as the painter, Georgia. (In the novel, Manuele, Georgia's husband, bears no resemblance whatever to Alan.)

During those years before 1940 I knew Elizabeth well, stayed often at Clarence Terrace, but I had not yet seen her in Ireland at Bowen's Court. So in a very important way I did not know her at all.

What I had come to know was the pattern of her life with Alan in London, where I felt like an adopted daughter. One takes so much for granted when one is young! I had never run a house, nor entertained, nor been responsible for ordering meals, and I had no idea what energy it all requires

—the devouring machine that someone has to keep running smoothly. In Elizabeth's life that machine had to be relegated to the periphery; central, of course, was her work. She worked extremely hard. No one saw her before one, and by then she had been at her desk for four hours. At one there was a break, lunch, and perhaps a short walk in Regent's Park just outside her front door. After that break she went back to her study for two more hours. At four or half past tea was brought up to the drawing room and intimate friends often dropped in for a tête-a-tête.

When Alan came home at half past five, the tensions subsided and everything became cozy and relaxed. He embraced Elizabeth, asked at once where the devil the cat was—a large fluffy orange cat—and when he had found her, settled down for a cocktail and an exchange about "the day." As in many successful marriages they played various games; Alan in his squeaky voice complained bitterly about some practical matter Elizabeth should have attended to, and she looked flustered, laughed, and pretended to be helpless. Alan's tenderness for her took the form of teasing and she obviously enjoyed it. I never saw real strain or needling between them, never for a second. Love affairs were a counterpoint. (Did Alan ever know? Strange to say, I believe he did not.) But the marriage was truly "home." And, what is possibly rare, no one was more aware of Elizabeth's genius than Alan. He knew passages from her novels by heart.

In London the Sunday ritual was to drive out into the country somewhere for a walk and a picnic lunch, followed by a long nap lying on the grass. On one occasion when I was with them, they looked, fast asleep, so much like figures on a tomb that I tried, to no avail, to wake Elizabeth by throwing small twigs at her. I myself can never sleep out-of-doors —there is too much going on.

When Elizabeth was out, Alan and I sometimes walked over to the zoo, making a beeline for the big cats. There before the abstracted gaze of a tiger or a panther Alan inevitably exclaimed, "Elizabeth!" Just now I unearthed a postcard of a tiger and murmured, "Elizabeth," for the resemblance is quite uncanny. I think it is the shallow-set small eyes and the long nose that do it—plus the somnolent power one always sensed under Elizabeth's purring laughter. Very occasionally she growled, but never in my presence roared. I cannot associate anger with her at all.

I did not go to Bowen's Court till after the war. In those days it was a twelve-hour flight. Elizabeth met me at Shannon, as she must have done many times each summer for her guests. After breakfast we drove the two hours through that incredible green world and after the sleepless night I reached Bowen's Court in a daze. The house stood at the lowest point of a bowl of rough grass where sheep lay about in white humps, a bowl walled in on the heights by plantations of trees, and as one came down the drive it loomed, gaunt, many-windowed, rather forbidding. It was forbidding partly because the facade was all glass and stone; there were no outside shutters to break the unrelenting expanse. And the stone was a bleak gray. Later on I saw how beautifully it took the changing light. But that first time, having expected something like an English Georgian house, I felt chiefly its isolation, only gentled by a huge round oak where sheep gathered for shade in front of the semi-circular terrace at the front door.

Inside, the enormous "hall" had become the dining room after Elizabeth inherited. There the family portraits hung against faded scarlet, and the great staircase at the end fanned out in two directions at the first landing. Except at mealtimes we lived in the library, Henry Bowen's study—

pale-brown velvet sofas, secretaries filled with his books, a wood fire, and in the center always a grand formal bouquet of flowers from the garden.

One of the pleasures at Bowen's Court was to go out after breakfast to pick. The garden, as in all these demesnes of the Ascendancy, was set apart, an acre perhaps enclosed in a brick wall too high to climb over; it contained vegetable plots as well as flower borders and often a greenhouse for fruit. It came to me as a shock to realize that the reason for the wall was to keep the Irish out. At Bowen's Court there was no greenhouse and, since the gardeners had had to be reduced to one old man, the garden was overgrown and helter-skelter. But there were still roses and perennials to pick. I see Elizabeth, slightly flushed, wandering about with a flat basket and scissors, totally absorbed, inventing, as she picked, the bouquet that then took an hour or more to construct for the library table.

My room was on the third floor, off The Long Room that extended the whole width of the house and had been designed as a ballroom, then never used because (it was discovered) the floor would not have borne the weight of a multitude dancing. Instead, it had become the playroom when Elizabeth was a child. All the rooms on this floor were low-ceilinged and felt warmer than those below. In mine I found a great bed covered with a crimson quilt; there were roses in a Lowestoft bowl on a table by the window. But of course what I did first was look out and drink in the silence, the great trees, the rough grassy slopes, and feel my way into an atmosphere that, at first, felt strange and a little lonely.

The house was austere, partly because of the high windows. At night one closed the shutters from inside; otherwise moths and bats flew in. (One of the things that "unnerved" Elizabeth completely was the large silent moths.)

The house was underfurnished, even bare in places, with few rugs. When it rained there was a chill in those high, darkened rooms.

That year there was still no running water. (Bathrooms were put in later after the success of *The Death of the Heart*.) Irish maids brought up hot water in jugs after breakfast and again before dinner; they brought tea early in the morning. All this was "home" for Elizabeth. All this became her; her physical presence took on its just proportions in the high rooms. She always seemed to me to be slightly more absentminded than usual at Bowen's Court, as though she were pulled down there into subterranean layers of memory, as though the subconscious came close to the surface there, and she was living many lives. As she herself said in her chronicle of the house, "The not long past of these houses has been very intense; no Irish people—Irish or Anglo-Irish—live a day unconsciously. Lives in these houses, for generations, have been lived at high pitch, only muted down by the weather, in psychological closeness to one another and under the strong rule of the family myth. . . . I know of no house in which, while the present seems to be there forever, the past is not pervadingly felt."

For Elizabeth the house had always been the heaven and haven after journeys that began when she was seven, journeys often made necessary by tragic events. She told me once, "It is very strange when the most terrible thing that can ever happen to you happens to you when you are thirteen." When Elizabeth was thirteen her mother died. They had been living on the South Coast, at Folkestone, then Hythe during the years of her father's breakdown; so Elizabeth was already in exile so far as place went, and had been deprived of her father. She was shunted off to school and put under the care of a maiden aunt, Aunt Laura. Elizabeth insisted on wearing a black tie with her school uniform. " 'My

Black,'" she says in the posthumous *Pictures and Conversations*, "was the last I had of my mother. *That* gone, there would be nothing so far as I knew, ever again. For I could not remember her, think of her, speak of her or suffer to hear her spoken of."

Elizabeth was thirty-one when she came back to Bowen's Court as the owner, came back for springs and summers with Alan (they were living near Oxford at the time), and could at last resume the continuity, resume roots that had been uprooted when she was still a child, and reached deep into the family history, take up again a long dream and make it real. Guests could not know that what looked so safe and grand was based on no financial security beyond what she and Alan earned. Few ever thought to buy liquor at Shannon or realized that they were drinking gin bought with very hard work.

When I first went to Bowen's Court everything in Elizabeth's life was opening out—she was on the brink of fame; she was in her glory as a woman, and the atmosphere was joyful, released. (I felt the strain much later after Alan's death.) We went on delightful expeditions to Mitchellstown for provisions and parked among hundreds of donkey carts, so one had a vision of rows of long ears, and could not help being aware that the demesne of Bowen's Court was not exactly Ireland, but the donkey carts surely were. We sometimes walked to the village, Kildorrery, to order sherry, sitting down at the counter for sips and tastings and much village gossip. Occasionally we drove considerable distances to visit neighbors among the gentry—Eddie Sackville-West was just over the border in Tipperary. The holiday atmosphere that prevailed was perfectly rendered, I think, by our odd sortie every afternoon to a neighbor's house in the village, a cottage, really, which had a bathroom. There we repaired, two or three of us, with towels and soap and a thermos of martinis, to chat and joke and to take turns having a bath. The contrast with austere Bowen's Court was amusing, and the walk back and forth half a mile or so under great trees was a delightful prelude to dressing for dinner.

The memories of that first visit flowered much later in my novel *A Shower of Summer Days*, in which the hero is the house itself, although the people who inhabit it are imaginary. Especially Violet bears no resemblance at all to Elizabeth, for Violet is the type of the English "lovely."

During the blitz Alan and Elizabeth had stayed in London, at Clarence Terrace. They were both air wardens, and at every alert went out into the total blackness, wondering whether they would ever see each other again. Once they returned to find the house cordoned off because an unexploded bomb had fallen on it. They were given a few seconds to take something out and Elizabeth rushed in and picked up a box of two hundred cigarettes, more precious at that time, she told me, than anything else she could lay her hands on. She was and remained a compulsive smoker. Occasionally they had a brief respite in Ireland—she has written in at least one story of what it was like to find the unbelievable lighted cities, plentiful food, no rationing, and the ambivalence toward the war, from which the Irish, as a government, had chosen to remain immune.

It is a strange thing to be born Anglo-Irish, to be so deeply rooted in a landscape, yet always to be considered an alien breed by its inhabitants. Yet the Anglo-Irish after four hundred years of the Ascendancy were no longer British and did not feel British. There was conflict. I remember how Elizabeth at one time suffered from the taunts of one man she loved who was Irish; there was never, there could not be, a perfect equilibrium after centuries of such hatred on one side and condescension on the other.

Possibly she felt at ease in the United States, where she

had many friends, because here at least she was free of those particular tensions. She was much warmer and more instinctual in her relations with strangers than the English as a whole allow themselves to be. She was willing to go deep into friendship in a few days or even hours if she felt an affinity, though she could be very distant if she did not. She was open to experience in a rare way, a way without snobbism, although she expected good manners, the amenities of social intercourse, to be maintained.

Sometime after the war she wrote me that she would love to come to see Judy and me in Cambridge, if I could arrange a lecture to pay her expenses from New York. The English department at Wellesley came forward, and at my suggestion Elizabeth talked about the short story as she herself approached it. It was a brilliant lecture, a lecture in which she made a statement I have pondered and found useful ever since: "If one is a writer one must regard oneself impersonally as an instrument."

For many years after that, Elizabeth paid her way to America with lectures. Unfortunately, for reasons unknown to me, she did not often choose to talk about her own practice either as novelist or short story writer, but preferred to give a formal written lecture about other writers such as George Eliot. I think this was a mistake. In a formal lecture the stammer became more of an impediment; members of an audience who did not know her personally have told me more than once that it made them frightfully nervous. But in conversation the stammer, far from being an infirmity, seemed always to give a curious emphasis to a phrase and was part of Elizabeth's charm. In a less formal lecture it might have had the same effect.

At any rate, that first lecture gave her confidence, and gave us the pleasure of having her with us for a few days. Our apartment on Oxford Street was anything but luxurious, but Elizabeth was wonderfully adaptable, a cozy guest. What fun we had arranging the flowers together before a small party we gave in her honor! That was the best of it, because it turned out to be a terribly stiff evening of the most deadly academic kind. The last thing Elizabeth wanted of a social occasion was that it be turned into a seminar on the art of writing, or that she herself be treated as a pundit. And I couldn't help comparing the atmosphere of this Harvard group with the merriment of their Oxford equivalents as I had seen them at Clarence Terrace. Harvard at that time did not represent the *gai scavoir*.

We saw Elizabeth nearly every year—later at Wright Street, where we closed off a small parlor for her as a work-room. Wherever she found herself, in a hotel, or as a guest in a private house, or in a college dormitory, Elizabeth worked as usual all morning. Writing provided a continuity, a means toward self-integration, I feel sure. That—and washing her white doeskin gloves, which were as much a part of her style as the fact that she rarely wore a hat.

But the time was to come, inevitably, when she would be taken from us. She had now become a lion as well as looking like one. And one day Alice James called me to apologize for "stealing Elizabeth" who, it appeared, was to stay with her on her impending visit. Alice gave splendid dinner parties and had a big house where Elizabeth could be far more comfortable than with us. There would be a maid to iron her dresses. (I see her still, standing before our iron-ing board in the cellar, having insisted that she could manage very well alone.) I did feel a little sad, for Elizabeth in Cambridge had been "our Elizabeth" till then. During her stay at Alice's Elizabeth called me one morning in quite an unnerved state because, she said, the physical comfort and space were spoiled by acute psychological discomfort and claustrophobia. Those necessary morning hours of concentra-

tion were constantly interrupted by an *affairée* Alice, wanting to know whether she would like so-and-so to be invited
for dinner, what she preferred for tea, and so on. I must
admit this call gave me a good deal of ignoble pleasure.

On another occasion when Elizabeth stayed near Boston
in a very grand house indeed, she found that her bedroom,
which had every luxury, lacked a writing desk! When will
kind hostesses understand that a writer must have a place
to write and without it feels like a fish out of water, gasping
for air, on however luxurious a bed and with however large
a bath at hand?

Elizabeth was now in her glory, and it is lovely that she
came into it long before her death and could enjoy it—especially an honorary doctorate from Oxford. But I think the
work by which she will live had been accomplished. It may
be that the blitz and the deep exhaustion following on so
many sleepless nights and such sustained tension over a
long period cost more than she knew at the time and reduced
what had seemed inexhaustible creative vitality. Some of
her best short stories came out of that London in peril, but
no novel written after the war comes up to *The House in
Paris* or *The Death of the Heart*, in my view. And only one,
A World of Love, had her signature of oblique romanticism
and poetry. In a letter to me from Rome she said, "I'm glad
A World of Love gave you pleasure. You can see why it's
deliberately such a short book. It's on the periphery of a
passion—or, the intensified reflections of several passions in
a darkened mirror. It was joy to write—natural (because
of the native naturalness of the setting) as no book of mine,
I suppose for a long time, has ever been."

I saw Elizabeth twice more in Ireland. The first visit in
July turned out a little differently than planned. At the air-
port Elizabeth told me that we were not going to Bowen's
Court because she had had to rent it for the summer to

make ends meet, and she was taking me instead to spend a few days at her aunt's—Edith Colley—near Dublin. I was excited at the prospect, for I had never met any of Elizabeth's family, and, besides, Elizabeth herself had spent a year at Clondalkin when she was seventeen, going to art school in Dublin; so it had been "home" for a while at a time when she was very much at a loose end.

Clondalkin is set among gently rolling fields, a park dotted with oaks, and it has, so much nearer a city, none of the stark grandeur of Bowen's Court. Besides, it had been lived in by large families and was warm, cluttered, a little dilapidated, full of Victorian furniture, children's tricycles in the hall, and altogether an extremely casual atmosphere. As Elizabeth's friend I was warmly welcomed by Edith Colley, a charming old lady with very blue eyes, who had her own parlor on the second floor, and lived there in the big house with her son and his wife and children. The son's passion was racing cars. I never did really "connect" with that generation, I'm afraid.

I was fascinated by all I saw around me. Clondalkin has a water garden, with a bridge over a shallow stream and lovely plantings of iris and other water-loving flowers on its banks. We were taken almost at once to visit the walled garden, where peacocks strutted on the high broken wall and screamed their desolate screams. It had all become a ruin and finally the Colleys had rented it out to a Dutchman, a market gardener, who showed us around, proud of his leeks and cabbages, opening the door to the greenhouse with a flourish to show off his peaches, just ripening there. But there was something sad about it—the overgrown dried-out pool in the center that had been a goldfish pool, the breaking up of formal flower beds. The Anglo-Irish are not having an easy time these days keeping estates going without gardeners and servants, hanging on by the skin of their teeth. It gave

me much to ponder—did their laissez-faire attitude stem
from the hard facts that there was so much in need of mending or care and so little help to be had that finally people
gave up trying? The racing car represented the new world.

But for me, of course, Clondalkin was full of the ghost of
young Elizabeth, going out to dances in Dublin, wanting
to be a painter. It is not strange that such a visual writer, one
might almost say such a painterly writer, began in another
medium. Might she have turned into a feminine Vuillard?

I did see Bowen's Court again, under strange circumstances—a disastrous visit which I recount here in order,
perhaps, to exorcise it. At first I was the only guest. I had a
different room this time, on the second floor, where the ceilings were high and drafts seeped in through the tall windows;
rain poured down; Elizabeth worked all morning of course,
and I wandered about rather at a loose end because it was
difficult to make a nest and settle down to work with icy
fingers. There was no Alan to spread his balm of kindness,
for he had died very suddenly in 1952 and this must have
been some years later when I myself was in a period of
transition, feeling my way toward finding a house of my own
in the country, a need for roots that had come upon me with
a strong compulsion after the death of my father and the
sale of his house in Cambridge. At Bowen's Court, too, there
was a feeling of ending, of obscure pressures and anxieties,
and Elizabeth seemed more absentminded than usual.

The mood and the atmosphere changed with the arrival
unexpectedly, after a phone call from London, of Miss Lovelace, a charming and beautiful young Californian who
arrived with all the flurry and excitement of the adorer who
has found her way to the promised land. If I had been a
little at a loose end before, I was now in double jeopardy
and had become what Elizabeth once called herself—"an

agitated observer" of a scene in which I clearly was expected to take no part, but which I recognized with a pang as the mirror image of my own first stays at Bowen's Court when I was the welcomed young adorer myself. I stayed in my room as much as possible but had to go down at cocktail time when it was usual for guests to gather in the library. But there, so intense was the exchange going on that I felt like an intruder, treated with bare civility. It was as acute a case of psychological discomfort as I have ever experienced.

The next day, our last—for Miss Lovelace and I both had early planes to take for London, and were to spend the night at Shannon—Elizabeth suggested a drive to see Spenser's castle, or what is left of it, Kilcolman Keep. I had never seen it, decided to go along, in spite of pouring rain, and took my place, like an unwanted governess, in the back seat. My corduroy raincoat was supposed to be waterproof but turned out to soak up water like a sponge. The "torn-open ruin," as Elizabeth has described it, is two or three hundred yards from the road on a desolate open plain. Getting wetter, I followed youth and splendor across the uneven turf. Sheer discomfort prevented my appreciating the romantic ruin. While Elizabeth, leaning on the parapet, spoke marvelously about Spenser, and Miss Lovelace glowed, water trickled down my neck; my coat had begun to feel like a leaden straitjacket, and I wished devoutly that I had stayed home.

Of course the whole scene is a perfect Elizabeth Bowen short story. How I wish I had seen her again and been able to talk about it! For Elizabeth was wonderfully sensitive to both the humor and tragedy of such "plights" and we might have laughed together and so healed the wound. But, for reasons I shall never now know, I had become a second-class citizen in Elizabeth's province. When I had not heard from her for several years I cabled a New Year message, and when that was never answered, I had to realize that our friendship had come to an end.

Had she, after all, minded my writing about Bowen's Court? A young scholar who came to talk with me about her suggested as much. Was that the reason, so that, for her, as a result of this literary invasion of privacy, I had in fact become an intruder? When I began to think about writing a portrait of Elizabeth, and was taking down her books from my shelves, a letter fell out dated January 11, and from its contents I presume that was January of 1953. In it she names a date when she would like to come and stay with Judy and me: "I am looking forward to being with you both more than I can SAY.

"Oh, and also, May, the joyful letter I have had all in my mind and heart about *A Shower of Summer Days* being so lovely never yet has got written. I read the book twice, and parts again. I do hope the book has made you as happy as it has made me and, I know, many others—When we meet, I can say, or try to say, what I did not write. You have done something so good in this novel, so strong, understanding and delicate. All my love, Elizabeth."

I read it and felt the balm slowly taking possession. For the last twenty years of her life I did not see Elizabeth. I did know that Bowen's Court had been sold and then later torn down by the new owners. Why? She had spoken to me once of the possibility that young cousins might buy it, but it was not after all to be kept in the family; she was the last of the Bowens of Bowen's Court. She bought a little house in Hythe, Hythe where she had lived with her mother as a child, where her father had joined them after his breakdown. And in 1974 she died of cancer, like her mother.

When people die, a circle is drawn around them and it is sometimes possible to see them whole, and defined, as is never possible during the flux and change of any life as it is being lived. But I find this hard to do in Elizabeth's case because she remained mysterious. The mystery, perhaps, lay in the fact that she was so open to experience on the surface, but below the surface few of her friends penetrated, though all must have sensed the tremor, earthquake, tension under her keen enjoyment of life moment by moment. It was this tension that gave her face its haunted, tragic look in repose, that kept her every relationship in suspense except perhaps that with her husband, and that, no doubt, provided the intense psychic climate of her work.

For me, so young and intolerably innocent when she came into my life, she was like a great landscape (one of those so full of mystery at the back of Renaissance portraits) to which I returned again and again, trying to define what made it so grand and so intimate, so full of nuance, irony, intelligence, wit, and at the same time so disarmed and disarming. The background is the Irish mountains of County Cork, the secret valleys, the rivers, and the great trees at Bowen's Court, but in the foreground there is a bewildering multiplicity of cities, and of people. I see her flushed and happy sitting in a café in Salzburg with Sean O'Faoláin; in a Greek restaurant in Soho where I lunched with her and Eudora Welty; in New York City, feeling her way nervously into a rented apartment; in Paris in a tiny elegant house; lying under a tree somewhere in Kent like a figure on a tomb; with Judy and me, having tea in Cambridge; but most of all stretched out on the Regency sofa at Clarence Terrace, a pillow behind her head, talking and laughing about T. S. Eliot's long calls late in the afternoon, how the tension was really unbearable by the time Alan came home to relieve it; and finally in the dusk of a late summer evening, standing in the long windows of her bedroom at Bowen's Court in an ecstasy of terror about the moths.

What she achieved, very much within the tradition of the English novel and short story, memorializes a rather closed society, that society that moved from the Anglo-Irish great houses to London and Oxford and back. But the Anglo-Irish are displaced people and Elizabeth's most moving work deals always in some way with the displaced. One thinks at once of her long story "The Disinherited," of the lovers in the dark bombed city, of the children in *The House in Paris*, and that most poignant of all the homeless, the young girl in *The Death of the Heart*. What looks like such a "safe" scene is proved not to be. To displaced people "place," the atmosphere of a house or a landscape, become haunting, as does the suspended moment in time, the last September before chaos begins. These are not subjects that will ever be exhausted or dated; they are too deep in the human consciousness. And although Elizabeth Bowen's work is now going through the brief eclipse that Virginia Woolf's did, I feel sure that she will eventually take her place in the continuity of English literature as an authentic genius. For is there anyone really at all like her? Is she not absolutely unique?

How did she influence me? Not, I think, as a writer. Virginia Woolf and Mauriac influenced me far more. But I immersed myself in her every work as it appeared with passionate interest and the slight irritation felt by the addict— that there is never *enough*. I was transported by her books, but I did not feel any real affinity with them so far as my own work was concerned. I have never belonged to a "society" as she so definitely and irrevocably did. But we are influenced inescapably and deeply by anyone so greatly admired and cherished.

I think Elizabeth helped tame the wild antisocial being I was at twenty-five. More than anyone else I have known she made me aware of social grace, the warmth and charm with which she made a dinner party flower, for instance.

But, more important than that, she taught me to be less intransigent and less demanding than I might have been without her. No one could be more sympathetic or illuminating about her friends' peccadilloes or plights in affairs of love, but she lived by a strong code, and though she herself was often "tortured" by people who loved her, she was never mean and never cruel. She once said something that I did not forget about what she considered a rather cavalier attitude on my part to a man who was in love with me, though it was said very gently.

She made it clear by her own life that it is possible to engage in extramarital affairs and keep one's dignity and one's personal truth intact, without hurting one's life partner. No small feat! It requires a mixture of adventurousness and discretion where feeling is concerned, discipline (yes), and an inexorable law that certain forms not be broken. The form, for Elizabeth, lay partly in her work and its unceasing demands, which she forced herself to meet every day, wherever she was and with whomever she was, and partly in behaving always "like a gentleman." But what haunts is her own statement in the posthumous *Pictures and Conversations* about her childhood stance after her mother died: "I registered what I loved with such pangs of love (that is to say, registered what was round me) only with an unwilling fraction of my being. This was the beginning of a career of withstood emotion. Sensation, I have never fought shy of or done anything to restrain." It is all that withstood emotion that lights up her work with its peculiar haunting mystery and power.

—Lotte Jacobi

Louise Bogan

ELEVEN

Louise Bogan

LONG BEFORE I ever saw her face to face Louise Bogan, both
as poet and critic, had been a key figure for me. I bought
The Sleeping Fury in 1937 when I was twenty-five and my
first book had just appeared. I can still remember the shock
and exhilaration it meant, how I pondered the poems—those
strict spare lines, where emotion was so often disciplined by
irony. And at a time when lyric poetry was becoming increasingly unfashionable, Bogan as critic was a cogent defender. Each *New Yorker* piece was a *piqûre*, so to speak.
"The great importance of keeping the emotional channels of
a literature open has frequently been overlooked. The need
of the refreshment and the restitution of feeling, in all its
warmth and depth, has never been more apparent than it
is today, when cruelty and fright often seem about to over-

whelm man and his world. For women to abandon their
contact with, and their expression of, deep and powerful
emotional streams, because of contemporary pressures or
mistaken self-consciousness, would result in an impoverishment not only of their inner resources but of mankind's at
large. Certainly it is not a regression to romanticism to remember that women are capable of perfect and poignant
song; and that when this song comes through in its high and
rare form, the result has always been regarded not only with
delight but with a kind of awe." That paragraph was written
in 1947 in a long essay "The Heart and the Lyre." How well
it defines Bogan's own genius!

Already in 1940 I had written to her on the whole subject
and received an answer, "What can be done concerning the
general distrust and even hatred shown toward lyric poetry,
so prevalent now, I can't think. Nothing, I suppose" . . . and
the letter ends, "The only thing to do is: do what one can,
and not sell out."

In 1943, inspired by the free concerts and readings going on
in London at the National Gallery during the blitz, I wondered whether it would not be possible to do something of the
sort in New York, where I was then working at OWI in the
film department. I first enlisted the support of the New York
Public Library (they offered a room once a week in the
evening) and then wrote to twelve or fifteen poets to ask
whether they would be willing to read as a gift to the public.
Among those who accepted were James Agee, W. H. Auden,
and Marianne Moore, but I was disappointed that Louise
Bogan refused, and troubled because the phrasing of the
refusal suggested that she was not well. She implied that she
felt unable to read anywhere. "The Poets Speak" took place
on six evenings in October and November of '43. In Louise
Bogan's selected letters only two letters written in '43 appear.
These speak of the illness of her father and anxiety about

paying his hospital bills. But I know from things Louise said to me later that there was a time of near despair in the '40s when none of her books were in print. For a writer to be unobtainable by readers is, of course, like being buried alive.

I did not meet her until ten years later, in the fall of '53. I had driven most of the night from Washington and arrived at 709 West 169th St. in a rather hallucinated state. It was a dilapidated apartment building and for a moment I couldn't find the name Bogan, then realized that Louise was still using her married name, Holden, though she had been divorced for many years. The apartment was on the sixth floor. I stood in the dingy hall for a moment before daring to push the button at her door. I knew that the meeting, for me, was momentous.

Then I remember vividly the sense I had of coming into rooms as intimate and revealing as a self-portrait. It was "Louise's place" from the big dining room table, strewn with papers, where she worked, to the living room it opened into. Here there were shelves and shelves of books, a sofa, chairs and small tables, the colors peacock blue and gray, I believe. There was nothing that looked interior-decorated, fashionable, or anything but simply beautiful and appropriate.

From the windows one caught a glimpse of the Hudson from beyond the tall Presbyterian hospital and it was quite clear at once by the way she showed it to me that this "piece of the river" was a kind of barometer of Louise's moods and at the same time a release from them. Then or later she often reminded me that Manhattan is an island. She liked to think of herself as not connected with the mainland, but an inhabitant of that special province, the city of New York. This intense awareness and taming of her immediate surroundings made me think of Marie Closset's rooms (the poet Jean Dominique) near Brussels.

I was deeply moved, more than I dared show. For here I

felt perfectly in my element, at home, and such sensations
I had until now associated only with Europe. What was the
magic formula? I have often wondered. Perhaps it was partly
that one sensed an intense inner life at work. It was an apartment where a poet lived alone, a woman lived alone. It
breathed an air of achieved calm. It was important, one
sensed, that things be in their places—a pretty ashtray, a
flower in a glass. And all this order and calm was humanized
by the piles of papers and journals, the pot of ink, the workful
disarray of the big table still in sight next door. (So great was
my feeling for what I first saw that day that I was dismayed
when a few years later Louise had a decorator help her make
it all a bit more stylish. For me the soul had gone out of it
then. It had become a guarded place that no longer gave its
inhabitant away.)

Louise was taller and larger-boned than I had expected.
She had good hands, hands suitable for someone who played
the piano as an avocation. But of course what magnetized
were the strange aqueous eyes, changing and transparent like
the sea, sometimes green, sometimes gray, always lucid. In
repose they were Irish-cold. But that day I saw a smiling
person, smiling a sometimes mischievous smile as when she
uttered the characteristic words, in response to my complaints about lack of recognition, "What is more ridiculous
than a successful poet?"

One of Louise's charms was the way she included an inter-
locutor, setting herself beside him or her as an equal, imply-
ing always an affinity, "you and I are the same breed, of
course." It was comforting, even when patently untrue. At
any rate, at that first meeting we laughed a lot, exchanged
views, as one does, about fellow poets and writers in general,
and found ourselves in almost total agreement. One exception
was Virginia Woolf, for Louise had been exasperated by what
had become a cult and there she was gingerly in her praise.

I had never had a poet friend except Jean Dominique in Belgium with whom I felt in such accord. I left her dazzled and intoxicated, with just a little point of doubt as to what she really felt about my work—and that doubt remained to the end.

As a consequence of that first meeting we exchanged letters more intimate than any of the later ones, for we were feeling our way into a friendship and needed to probe what would be possible for us and what would not be possible. An *amitié amoureuse*? Here Louise treated me with the utmost tact, generosity, and respect. She did so by warning me almost at once of what she called "a psychic flaw" which had to do with her relation to her mother, The Sleeping Fury of that poem, who must have made her feel as a child that she was living in the eye of a storm. Any relationship with a woman, not purely friendship, risked bringing back trauma. She was deeply and no doubt rightly afraid. So the key to our relationship became a line of Yeats's that I can hear her voice saying now on the telephone as well as seeing it before me often at the ending of a letter, "She bade me take life easy as the grass grows on the weir."

And she wrote in one letter, "I do not say that you offer complications but I somehow felt that part of you is elsewhere; and now you tell me I am right in this. I think I can help you break through into more emotional freedom than you now have (emotional certitude) by just standing by, with my hand out . . ." and in another letter, "Remember that I proffer you all that I can proffer any human being. Which isn't, I suppose, v. much; but all of it is fresh and real and *non-patterned*."

I did at least have the wit to know how lucky I was and to believe, as was proved true, that our friendship would become stable and joyful and lasting. It went through several phases, as all friendships do—more fervent at the start, tougher and more critical on both sides as time went on. But the beginning in those first weeks of long letters (I was living in Cambridge and got to New York rarely) laid a solid foundation. Our meetings were always "occasions." Once in a while Louise made a shrimp salad, a speciality of hers, presented as "a work," as indeed it was, for she was really not a domestic person. More often we went out to a restaurant nearby which had marvelous crabmeat in a special sauce. We drank a lot, laughed, talked about everything under the sun, preferably hilarious adventures of a minor sort we had each had since the last time, and, of course, always literature in its every aspect. We had lively but never acrimonious arguments, and we quite simply enjoyed ourselves. Once we set out in my little Austen for the Brooklyn Botanical Gardens. I managed to get off the West Side Drive too soon and we found ourselves in a jumble of market carts and hooting trucks. Suddenly there was a mild crash. I looked out and saw a huge horse's head at Louise's window, a terrifying apparition. The car, I found, had been dented, but I was much too agitated to complain. Besides, we were both laughing hysterically because of Louise's poem,

> O God, in the dream the terrible horse began
> to paw at the air, and make for me with his blows.°

On another occasion we were so absorbed in trying to remember the whole of Housman's "I to my perils / of cheat and charmer" that I missed the exit off the George Washington Bridge and we ended by crossing it three times before we had caught the missing word of the poem and I had discovered where to turn off. Being with Louise, the most life-enhancing person imaginable, gave everything a zany charm, even disaster. Also, like me, she preferred small occasions

° Louise Bogan, "The Dream," from *The Blue Estuaries*.

to great ones—a short walk in Fort Tryon Park, a leisurely luncheon in a good restaurant, a "little drive," these were our pleasures. So sophisticated in matters of taste and literary judgment, Louise as a person was not sophisticated at all, totally unspoiled and unworldly. "Not bad," she would say with a smile, when some new honor came to her, "for a little girl from Roxbury, Mass." The Irish girl had an unerring eye for the pretentious in any sphere and could demolish it with the lift of an eyebrow. Perhaps one of our affinities lay in the fact that we were both "outsiders," observers of the social scene, never a part of it.

About once a year Louise would decide that the time had come for a holiday, a time to leave the island of Manhattan for a week or so. In the days when I first knew her, a holiday meant going to Swampscott, just north of Boston, to a boardinghouse where she lived in the plainest of rooms and took her meals out, where she was right on the shore and could walk along the boulevard (so reminiscent of European watering places), watching the waves come in and break on the sand, or sit on the rocks behind the house where she lived and look up at the pattern of acacia leaves against the sky. There an old school friend, Rufina, joined her for little expeditions to antique shops, and there I usually went down at least once to take her out for dinner. The great fun was to prepare a kind of magic basket (it was meant to carry wine and had four compartments) to take her, with a bottle of Scotch, a bunch of garden flowers in a jar, a new English book perhaps, to make her austere lodgings a bit more comfortable.

About material things Louise was a true poet, in that she lived well and even brilliantly on the minimum of comfort. As she put it herself in a letter, "As for my eight sided heart, which you question, dear May, I can only say that the octagonal here is somehow symbolic of freedom. Love

of things, I suppose, understood, more than love of human
beings. The delight in objects, both natural and artifacts,
which has grown in me ever since the *obsessive* person was
left behind (or buried, if you like, in the lowest layer of the
dream). The delight of the collector, which you sensed in my
room; the delight of the naturalist (which I never had when
young, except in flashes, but which makes me scrutinize
everything, from flowers to rocks on the shore, in these later
years); the delight of the amateur in the arts (the piano and
embroidery)."

The fates were kind in opening a door to a collaboration
I would not have dreamed of when we first met. In August
of '55 Louise informed me, "I started off the morning by copy-
ing out a work of yours! You will remember the rough draft
you did of 'Palme'? Well, I met Jackson Matthews and his
wife, last Thursday evening, and spoke to him of your very
real success. He was v. interested indeed." Jackson Matthews
was editing the complete Valéry in translation for the
Bollingen Foundation and had been searching for someone
to do the poems. Apparently he misunderstood and thought
Louise had done the version of "Palme" herself. At that point
he suggested a collaboration and in February of 1956 Louise
had a conference with the powers at Bollingen. "Mr. Barrett
is really very excited, and exceedingly hopeful about our
collaboration. He evidently considers the fact that you can
get the *feel* and *music* of Valéry over into English, as a sort
of Heaven-sent find." So it was all decided. We split $100 a
poem, which seemed munificent. But actually the work was
exceedingly difficult. I often sat at my desk from eight P.M.
to two A.M. like a spider weaving and unweaving an intricate
web.

Our method was that I translated the poem into form by
myself—this Louise could not do, as she frankly admitted.
Then she "scrutinized," as she put it, the result. She could

look at the English version with far more detachment than
I, who had been struggling with hundreds of alternatives
and in the heat of battle sometimes committed absurdities.
French is rich in rhyme; English very poor. Valéry is the poet,
par excellence, whose sound and meaning can hardly be
separated at all. The danger, constantly present, was that to
achieve one, one might distort the other. Louise did not
know French very well, and I, fluent, but no scholar, did not
know it well enough—I could have done better, perhaps, with
a French collaborator. But I believe the truth is that translation of poetry is better done by one person; if the translation
is to become an English poem, one person's taste and skill
alone should be at work.

Nevertheless we had a fine time, for months, meeting
every two weeks in New York, to go over what I had done
in the interval, laughing till we cried at certain absurdities
we (or I) had perpetrated, struggling over a single word for
half an hour, playing the fascinating game for all it was
worth. I learned a lot, of course. Who could help it between
Valéry and Bogan? Louise was very pleased with the results; she even suggested that we might get the Légion
d'Honneur from France—a grand illusion, but it delighted
me to witness her childlike pleasure in the prospect, she so
ironic usually about "prizes and honors."

Unfortunately our dream was shattered a year later when
Jackson Matthews wrote me to explain that, after long con-
sideration, he and the board at Bollingen had decided to
print the poems in French, accompanied by a literal prose
translation. I believe they were right. The best of what we
did was good, but it was not possible to do a comparable
poem in English in every instance. So the collaboration ended
with some of our translations being published in *Poetry*,
Metamorphosis, and *The Hudson Review*, and that was that.
We had no regrets. It had given us happy workful hours

together, and a goodly amount of pocket money too to spend on flowers. Best of all, it had given me the chance to see Louise at her very keenest and best, as she was when working, and I watched the intellect, the humor, and above all her sense of what poetry is, her poetic wisdom, one might call it, all functioning together.

My father died in 1956. In 1958, having sold his house in Cambridge, I bought and moved into an old farmhouse in Nelson, New Hampshire, not far from the MacDowell Colony where Louise was beginning to go for a few weeks each year. I moved in in October. Céline Limbosch, my mother's old friend, then in her seventies, and, after my parents' death, the person nearest to family in my life, announced that she was coming over from Belgium by freighter to help me settle in. I invited Louise to join Judy (with whom I had lived in Cambridge), Céline, and me for a housewarming on the October 12 weekend. I have never before or since had so many people together under my roof, and for the rather un-domesticated person I was then, it was daring. But I was intoxicated by my new life and wanted to share it. Céline teased me quite a lot because I was so nervous. She suggested that I might as well have been preparing to receive a queen— the truth was that Louise was not a very easy guest. I moved out of my bedroom so that she could be assured of privacy, for she groaned and sighed in her sleep and was, naturally, shy about being overheard. And in her nice, quiet, unassuming way she was demanding. Louise was to be dropped off at the house by friends, en route further north. It did not help that they were very late, and then drank so many martinis that by two P.M. I was forced to invite them for lunch. Louise on special occasions became anarchic, partly because she drank a martini down as though it were a glass of water and demanded another at once. After a third, she was knocked out and sometimes even fell asleep. I did mind

that the carefully prepared occasion was turning into a
shambles, but Céline remained fascinated by this curious
example of American *mœurs*, and was clearly enjoying
herself. Finally the guests took off and the rest of us went off
for naps to our several rooms.

Later, after a reviving cup of tea, I suggested that we do
as planned—go for a walk. I had it in mind to "walk the
boundaries," without realizing exactly what this implied
through ragged New Hampshire woods and brush, and
broken-down stone walls, and over ancient dumps full of tin
cans! We set out bravely, I in the lead with my pruning
saw, to cut a way through when necessary. Céline stayed
with me, but Judy and Louise gradually vanished behind us.
Occasionally we heard a shout and shouted back, "This way!"
But I had begun to be disoriented and was by then absorbed
in trying to find the way to the brook, the southern boundary.
There were brambles and fallen trees to cross. Gigantic
granite leftovers from the Ice Age loomed up. But at last I
broke through and there was the brook, lovely and alive,
rushing among stones, under tall pines, and we were walking
on soft pine needles. But where were the others? We heard
faint cries. Louise had sprained an ankle—or so she thought;
it turned out to be less severe than imagined. And I realized
when she and Judy emerged, flushed and exhausted, to join
us and walk the last mile up a dirt road, thank heaven, that
I had unwittingly put poor Louise through an experience
tantamount, for her, to climbing Mt. Everest without a
Sherpa in sight! The next morning she announced with evident surprise, "I seem to be all right."

I hope our drive then under canopies of gold with gold
above our heads and even under our wheels, as I turned off
onto dirt roads, exploring, and came to lonely farms, or a
sudden great view of Mt. Monadnock, dark blue, standing

over rolling pasture and the brilliant blue pocket of a lake, made up for the ordeal of the day before.

After Louise left, in the few days while Céline was still there, digging out a border for me in front of the house, helping me stack a load of wood, we talked of course about the visitation. Céline, who had met Louise simply as a friend of mine and knew how much I admired her, felt that Louise had been not very kind. That was not a true observation. Louise was kind but she was not warm. She could, however, be definite and forthright when there was real need. When, a few years later, I went through severe depression, it was she who forced me finally to make the decision to get help, who wrote to her own doctor, and obtained the name of someone I could see in Boston.

Her detachment, what seemed sometimes "unkind," was part of her armor, necessary for survival. One must see her spotlighted against a terrifying darkness that was always there in the background and that, at least three times in her life, required her hospitalization. It took me a long time before I understood how carefully she must design each day to keep the demon at bay, how carefully she must balance any emotional expenditure against possible disaster. Her life-enhancing qualities were often defenses, carefully placed and designed "snow fences," such as those New Englanders dispose to keep the snow from drifting dangerously and cutting off roads. In this our temperament and our problems were very different, as she had written me in 1954, "It all comes down to the fact that our deepest attitudes (toward life, toward the universe) are slightly different. I have been *forced* to learn to wait, to be patient, to wait for the wheel to turn. You are by *nature* impatient and drastic. I have been *forced* to find a way of loving my destiny; of not opposing it too much with my will. I have been *forced* 'to forgive life' in order to get through existence at all. If all these pressures have been put upon me, it must be for some reason; and my 'peace' and 'calm' are, as I have said again and again, too hard won to be lightly tossed aside."

During the years at Nelson I saw Louise whenever she was at the Colony for a few weeks. We had at least three afternoons of work polishing up the Valéry translations we wanted to publish in magazines, and we kept in touch by letter always. I became increasingly concerned after 1958 about her underlying depression, the struggle to keep afloat, and the fact that her primary energy as a writer was still going into reviewing for *The New Yorker*. In 1958 Louise was sixty and for a long time she had written no poems, or very very few, slight, and occasional ones. She talked quite often about "the long prose thing," which was, I gather, autobiographical, but I have no idea whether she actually wrote many pages of it. I felt that if she could have a year off from *The New Yorker*, a kind of sabbatical year, a great deal might happen. But when I suggested this to Katharine White, my own editor at *The New Yorker*, the answer was that it would be too great a risk—Louise might not get the job back.

It is not a good idea, really, for any one person to remain in such a position of power as that of poetry critic for *The New Yorker* for more than ten years, and Louise had been there for at least thirty. In the last years she noticed very few young poets and devoted the few pieces she did to old laureates like Auden, Marianne Moore, the Sitwells, Roethke—and consistently ignored others, such as Muriel Rukeyser. I felt this unfair but above all unfair to her own genius. One need only imagine what it must be to have every book of poems published pile up week by week to realize that such a weight stifles any impulse of one's own. It must feel like being buried under rubble.

The honors Louise had waited for for a long time now began to arrive, honorary degrees, membership first in the Institute of Arts and Letters, the Bollingen Award which she shared with her old friend, Leonie Adams, and a few months before she died she was elected to the Academy of Arts and Letters. She was beginning to be in great demand for lectures and short-term visits to colleges and universities. And I felt sure she could make up *The New Yorker* salary, never large, since she wrote only three or four pieces a year, without much trouble. True, *The New Yorker* is infinitely protective of its "regulars"; medical bills are often paid; severance was bound to be costly in anxiety, and even panic. But, long before she made the decision to leave, I had needled her about it. I felt that she had achieved a life-style that did, to some extent, keep the demons at bay, but at the expense of what really mattered.

Any poet knows that the muse cannot be commanded and nothing like a lyric poem is ever written out of a wish to write one. Poems erupt. For instance, Louise told me in a letter, "'The Daemon' was written one afternoon almost between one curb of a street and another." Even more extraordinary is the genesis of "Song for the Last Act." The poem reads like the culmination of a long passionate love affair, but was actually inspired by Louise having sat next to T. S. Eliot at a dinner party! Poetry is anarchic, but it is possible that it needs air and space to breathe in. I felt that Louise was allowing too many small jobs to clutter up that space.

And I was driven to complaints because I was increasingly aware that under her far greater fame and security than when I had first walked into her apartment, the undertow of depression was growing stronger. How is one to know? All I knew was that time was running out for the poet. All I knew was the darkening mood. Sometimes when I telephoned from Nelson, there were ten or twelve rings before there was an answer. Louise's voice sounded as though it were fading in (instead of fading out) from very far away, as though she had been drowning. Sometimes, by the end of our conversation, she sounded like herself again, but often I felt chilled when I set the receiver down.

I would be less than honest if I did not admit that I had been hurt and baffled by her failure to recognize me in *The New Yorker*. I never asked her to do so, of course, but she knew how long I had waited for an accolade from a peer. And when *The Land of Silence* came out she told me that she would review it. She built up a lot of suspense about that review, telephoned me when the proof came in, but said it would be bad luck to let me see that, I must wait till the piece appeared. Naturally, by then I anticipated a full review. It was a shock to discover that all this laying on of hands had ended in a few lines at the end of a review on Edith Sitwell! There were tensions between us in the last years, tensions that could not be talked about for obvious reasons.

On the surface, Louise, the charming companion for a walk and a talk and a drink, seemed open and at ease with herself and the world, but under that acquired layer of "wise living" she was hermetic. And the tragedy was that the hermetic part of her was locked into what her analyst had called "pathological faithfulness." In spite of at least two love affairs, one exceedingly happy, the source of poetry had been buried alive with her divorce from Raymond Holden. She spoke of this to me many times. After two martinis, Raymond's name always floated up in her conversation. We often talked about "imitation poems," the poems that do not come from the primary source, but are made out of more superficial experience by sheer craft and art. But the whole point was, as Louise herself felt, that sometimes "imitation" poems may open the door into authentic ones.

One must not forget that Louise Bogan was of Irish
blood, for she never forgot it. She had flashes of Irish malice
occasionally as well as Irish wit (directed against pretension
of any kind), and the brooding Irish was in her sea-green
eyes. The ocean, "the blue estuaries," were in her blood—
and a born suspicion of the Anglo-Irish, with the exception of
Yeats, "the greatest poet Ireland has ever known." The very
few times I heard her in passionate speech on a political
matter was about the persecution of the Irish in the days of
the Ascendancy. Otherwise she was apolitical and offended
(as many people are) by political poems, as rhetoric, not
from the primary source.

But if there were tensions between us, there was also
deep respect and affection. Even when we disagreed violently, I can re-read no letter from her without realizing
freshly how much she taught me. For she treated me as an
equal, and, in times of trouble, that forced me to straighten
my back. Here is a letter, for example, written in May 1954:
"I'm sorry you are exhausted, and even somewhat depressed.
The *U.S. Book Review* notice probably didn't help . . . But
it is a specimen example of one kind of criticism (academic),
and you should treasure it as such! As soon as we put pen
to paper we lay ourselves open to all sorts of humiliating, as
well as inspiriting, experiences; and we become true 'pros'
when we accept everything as it comes, and for what it is. We
must have at least one period in our careers in which everything seems overtaxing and completely difficult: this is the
sort of period which heralds change and growth, and we can't
duck it—if we do, we're done for, permanently. Edna Millay
tried to escape it, and spent years fumbling around for a
solution that just a little humility and grief, spent in the
right places, would have given her. Writing, at some central
point in the career, must present to us almost insuperable
obstacles; Yeats speaks of this point more than once. *I* am

in such a period for a *second* or *third* time; you may be in your initial one. So suffer and fight it through, dear May! You will have almost inexhaustible drive and energy. . . .

"It was of your 'delightful energy' that Marianne spoke, at Leonie's party . . . how you 'flew in' (or out, or around), with your 'pretty coat and distinctive hair'—such a contrast to the grim New Englanders which M. seemed to sense all around her."

Louise had another period of serious depression and was hospitalized for some weeks in the fall and winter of '65 but was home again in January '66, "the graph of post-depression rises v. slowly, and proceeds through areas of minor ills. Mornings remain rather grim, while afternoons and evenings clear up. The mysterious ways of the psyche!—But I am free from tranquilizers, and from the desperate hours known last spring and summer."

I did not see her in the last year of her life but those who did, notably Elizabeth Roget, who lived across the river and came over every week or so, began to be anxious. It becomes clear that the winter equinox was a dangerous time, as it is for most sensitive human beings. "The turn of the year" is in many ways the darkest time, literally, since the shortest day is in late December, and subconsciously we are going down into the darkness of which all the myths tell, that darkness before the rebirth of spring. Elizabeth Roget became very anxious when, during the whole month of December while she herself was away at the MacDowell Colony, she had no word from Louise at all. "I called her—January third —and heard the alteration in her voice, and noticed a sort of drifting of her mind. Afterwards there was only now and then a spark of the old Louise, and I could have wept for all that was lost."

Ruth Limmer chose, for good reason no doubt, to say nothing about Louise's death in her release of her letters,

What the Woman Lived, except that she died alone in her apartment in the small hours of February 4, 1970, of a coronary occlusion. Since there was no autopsy, this is the supposition. She does not choose to tell us that it was Elizabeth Roget who had the terrible shock of finding Louise that afternoon. "She had fallen out of her bed, face down, and the foot of the bed was shoved aside, and the chair at the head, piled with books, was thrown wide, and the books scattered." The last poem in Louise Bogan's last book is "Masked Woman's Song":

> Before I saw the tall man
> Few woman should see,
> Beautiful and imposing
> Was marble to me.
>
> And virtue had its place
> And evil its alarms,
> But not for that worn face,
> And not in those roped arms.*

Whatever the end for genius, have we the right to smooth over in any way the struggle to survive, the courage that that always demands? None of it, from the beginning in Livermore Falls as an Irish Catholic child living with an overpowering mother's rages, had been easy. Not the necessity to bring up an only child alone after her first husband died, nor to make a living from literary journalism. ("How hard I worked in the twenties," Louise says when she is gathering together a book of criticism.) Not the disaster of her second marriage and the slow and painful exorcism of the "obsessive person" of that marriage, nor the recovery from grief. Not the long years after Maidie, her daughter, was grown up when Louise learned to live

* Louise Bogan, *The Blue Estuaries*.

alone. Not, above all, the fear of breakdown and the three terrible experiences of it. ("Dear May, how wonderful it is to be unburdened by depression once more! To be at the mercy of that *oppression* is one of the most frightful experiences possible.") No, it was not easy to die alone, struggling for what we shall never know. It was exceedingly difficult to be Louise Bogan, and the triumph is perhaps in exact proportion, the other side of a diptych. On the one side much darkness, *"dunkel ist die Liebe, dunkel ist der Tod . . ."* and on the other an extraordinary rare light.

Just now when I opened my copy of *The Blue Estuaries* a thin blue page fell to the floor. I lay it here with love.

Holograph, "One of May's Bouquets"

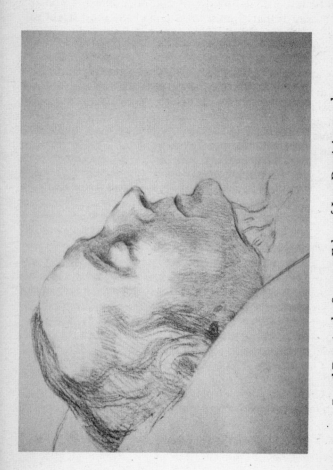

Pencil Drawing by Suzanne Fabry of Jean Dominique on her
deathbed

TWELVE

Jean Dominique

In *I Knew a Phoenix* I have spoken of Marie Closset, and of her school, the Institut Belge de Culture Française where I studied for a year as a child, of her brief written criticisms of my themes, and of the sense of mystery that surrounded her. I am to speak here of someone so different from that austere and distant presence, someone so close to my inwardness over a period of more than twenty years, that perhaps the only way to do so is to name her by her other name, the name she had chosen for herself as a poet: Jean Dominique.

Those who had known her first as a teacher of genius, and known the atmosphere of extreme reserve, of dedication, with which she protected herself, came in the last years to know the unguarded "Jean-Do" whose huge gray eyes could penetrate, even when they had gone blind, to the very center of one's consciousness, whose light small hands seemed always to be dispensing treasures, whose love grew more tender and more aware as one reason for existence after another was taken from it; "Jean-Do" who remained a child, a poet, a lover, and sometimes a sad clown—that "Gilles" of Watteau's, all in white, whom she had chosen for her Muse—until the very end.

I am not to speak here of the intellectual mastery, of the standards she had held up with such formidable and pitiless authority. But that side of her nature and of her influence is very much in my mind, because it is what gave peculiar sweetness to the being I knew, and we all knew in the last years, when it seemed as if every layer of pride and reserve were peeled off one by one like the skins of an onion, until what was left was nothing but a translucent center as alive to light or shadow, to a caress, to a passing bird, as is a child or a very old woman of genius.

How this was achieved will always remain a mystery, but it is that journey into old age and death which she made alone that lies before me like some great final lesson: she who taught us so much taught us finally how to die.

Part of it was the art of memory, the continual nourishment she found in tasting over and redesigning the past in the intimate essays she wrote for the Brussels *Soir* when she was in her late sixties:

> " 'Le temps s'en va, le temps s'en va, Madame,
>   Las! le temps non, mais nous nous en allons . . .'

"How curious it is to find oneself saying, 'Fifty years ago!' . . . One cannot get used to the idea. One has to smile, as one says it, as if it were a matter of a joke, a game, or a pretence. But no, it is simply life passing. One was absent-minded, one thought of oneself as young; one felt the warm sun of afternoon still on one's cheek . . . and it is already evening, and it is almost night.

"Fifty years ago . . . Ah, yes! Let me quickly seize a fleeting image that is shaping itself behind my eyelids; let me press it gently there before I let everything go. It is the face of childhood, of that silent time, when one utters nothing, but when at the end of the day one has burned so many desires in the crucible of dreams that one finds oneself as reduced as sand, as light as ash."

And if this was true of Marie as a child, how much more true of Jean Dominique! There was no diminution in the intensity of all that she burned in herself each day, only it became more and more refined into light, into ash. Nothing was lost, but some things were transformed; the bitterness that cries out in many of the poems, that bitterness that she called "also a kind of nourishment," was transformed into something more active than acceptance, an angelic humor and the quick leap of fantasy into the breach: "I walk leaning on Blanchette's arm, the arm that has found its place under mine again as when we were twenty and our hearts were completely Russian! A friend has made for me a perfectly Tolstoyan fur hat in which I intend to present myself at Heaven's gate like a faithful *moujik* of the old days, especially that one who had the same understanding with his horse Moukhorty as he did with God."

"When they were twenty" they had walked each other home from the Ecole Normale arm in arm, Marie going miles out of her way, her feet wearing the wings of passion, only, when she finally reached home, to write a twenty-page letter to say all that had not been said. Later, when Blanche Rousseau married, Marie Closset went to live with Marie Gaspar; and finally when Blanchette's husband died and the school was built, she too came to share the end of her life with her two old friends in the rosy brick house on the Avenue de l'Echevinage in Uccle. There I knew this remarkable trio. There I described them, too early, and in the first rapture of discovery, in my first novel. Now I may call them by their own names: "Is it time? I'm afraid it is time to say that these are three old ladies. They are called The Little Owls; why nobody knows, but for thirty years they have been called The Little Owls, though nothing could be less like an owl than any one of them, as they are always in bed by nine o'clock. Jean-Do is tiny and delicate, with enormous eyes behind dark glasses, which she slips on and off as if she were hiding behind them (and she is), thin fair hair like a boy's, a small strange face, that can look very severe when her eyes are hidden. She is a poet.

"Blanchette is the beauty—pigeon-white curly hair, brilliant blue eyes, now always ringed in shadow, delicate hands with a wedding ring on. She is all charm. People say of her, 'She must have been a great flirt.' She loves bonbons, but is not allowed them any more; and silks that rustle, and bows, and flowers on her dresses, but she cannot afford them.

"Gaspari has a lean eager face, bright eyes like a bird's, fuzzy gray hair in a fringe and drawn to a knot on top. She is the clown of the family, spirited, intense, quick-tempered —she cares for the other two with all the swiftness and precaution of a mother bird."

It is this flowering of their lives together that Jean-Do offered like a bouquet in a letter to an old friend facing chronic illness: "O my little one, we can still invent a charming life for you, a little reading, a little music, a handful of tender friends who will come rarely, and the house of l'Echevinage where I shall wait for you with Blanchette and Gaspari to amuse you with our old foolishness and our hearts that are still children, and so many memories to share, and to exchange, and to caress."

I don't suppose anyone ever walked up through the two lines of hydrangeas and stopped under the lovely oval fanlight of the front door without a moment's hesitation before ringing the bell. I don't suppose anyone ever penetrated the silent house which smelled of books and roses and Blanchette's rare cigarettes, without knowing that he was about to enter a charmed circle.

When I was a child in the school I never penetrated to the upper floor—that I did first when I was twenty-six and Jean Dominique was sixty-five; there were thirty-nine years between us. Yet from the first afternoon when I sat for hours on the small hard sofa by the window in her study and we talked of poetry, of ourselves, of everything under the sun, we found together once and for all what was to be an uninterrupted communion until her death. Time did not exist.

I had brought her my first book of poems. Although she could not speak English, she could read it and treated me at once as her peer. Here was the first real accolade I ever had from a poet, except that of Conrad Aiken on whose recommendation Houghton Mifflin had decided to publish my poems. I had loved Jean Dominique's poems long before I knew her except as a distant presence in the school, and, strangely enough, even before I was born, my father had loved them. One of her first books I have in my library is inscribed "George Sarton, 18th September 1904"! She was published by the Mercure de France and at that time had quite a reputation, but when I came to know her as a friend she had not published for many years. I think that my work became for her almost like a second flowering of her own, and that meant that she could get inside it both as lover and critic as no one else in my life ever has.

She too had loved both men and women, and often found her muse in a woman. I never had to explain anything to her about myself. She knew and had experienced it all. Only there was a great difference, an enriching difference, in our temperaments. She had had to lead in the later years an extremely restricted life because of frail health. In her youth she had traveled—to Venice, to the South of France, to Paris, to Ireland—but now she rarely left Brussels and her orbit became more and more the house, the garden, the village of Uccles, and the park with its great trees a few steps away. Her journeys were her visitors, and one or another of her many friends came every day. Her adventures had become these visits, and they were all in depth.

I, on the other hand, was at a stage of life where everything was opening out, in my work, in my friendships and love affairs, and in traveling back and forth from Europe to America nearly every year. The exchange was vivid between our two lives. The exchange was full of surprising recognitions—a part of what I might become seemed to be foretold in her life, and a part of what she had been was being played out again by me. Now that I lead a life of solitude myself, it has become even more clear how much I learned from her about how it can be achieved, and what large spaces a life that seems restricted may contain.

We wrote to each other at least once a week for twenty years, so that even when I did not see her for months at a time, I was in close touch with what she was reading and thinking and found myself in writing to her constantly evaluating what was happening to me. In a way it was a little what I do now in keeping a journal and perhaps I keep a journal because there is no one any longer to whom I could write such letters.

Our communion was an essence and changeless. But as the years went on, I came to understand differently and better how delicately balanced was the magic circle these three drew around them, and how much of its magic was a conscious creation. At best, a relationship of three people is precarious. This one was possible at all because of the peculiar grace of each member of it, the constant abdication of pride and self-sufficiency for the sake of each other. Gaspari had elected herself the support and protector of the other two, had long ago taken on the job of nursing Jean-Do during periodic attacks of the dreaded *vertiges*, when for days at a time the walls whirled around her and the pain was so acute that she screamed. She suffered from a rare form of epilepsy; the usual "fits" were replaced by terrifying pain in her head.

For a long time I regarded Marie Gaspar as the rock on which the other two leaned: this was one of the myths Jean-Do's understanding made possible, an understanding so delicate toward others, so ruthlessly demanding toward herself that it was a very long time before I suspected that Gaspari's need to feel useful, her image of herself as the faithful workhorse, was only part of the truth. That it was not quite the whole truth only proves once more what Jean-Do said to me once, with an angelic smile, when I protested something or other rather too righteously. *"Pourquoi avoir raison?"* she asked in that gentlest of mocking voices that could probe so deep. Why be in the right, indeed? What could be more foolish? one instantly recognized.

But if the superficial truth was more complex and difficult than it seemed, the deep truth of their relationship was that each depended on the other, and the fabric of their lives, three woven into one, made it impossible to disentangle who bore the heaviest responsibility. Certainly for many years Blanchette was the particularly cherished one, partly because of her beauty, partly because of her prestige as a writer and as a personality of immense magnetism. It does not matter now. What matters is to recognize that the magic circle implied an exacting exercise of the heart, a creation, a poem, if you will, affecting those who were lucky enough to be included in it, as poetry does. It harmonized and consoled.

In one of Jean Dominique's poems there are two lines that haunt me because they provide a glimpse into the inner world where she must, as did her two companions, suffer

alone, a glimpse into the dark side of a life frustrated in so
many ways, and triumphantly realized at the same time:

"O vieillesse qui viens, je crierai à Toi
Pour renoncer enfin à tout ce que je n'ai pas!"

She was in her late forties when she made that cry of re-
nunciation. The cruel irony is that in the final twenty-eight
years of her life she had to renounce not what she had never
had, but everything she had, every element in her life which
nourished her, everything that had made that life possible
at all. She must, as it were, give up her powers, one by one,
give up her sense of herself, and learn to depend on others
for everything. That she did this with such angelic humor,
patience, and lightness, that we who loved her were hardly
aware that anything had changed, is one of the miracles she
was able to perform.

First she lost her eyes, those eyes which had been such
faithful sources of strength, the light of the mind, those eyes
by which she read Tolstoy and the poets she loved, those eyes
on which her livelihood depended. It was, fortunately a slow
process. For years they could, in certain lights, at certain
times of day, and if she was not overtired, still discern the
features of a beloved face; and later, when she had ceased to
be able to read print, they could somehow still decipher a
letter if the ink was black enough; for half an hour at a time
there might be enough light in them to write a few pages.

And in the early years of the oncoming darkness
Blanchette was there to sit beside her and to read aloud. The
letters say it all: "The garden drenched in wet grass seems
a hundred years old. Blanchette is reading me *The Plague*.
The first chapter suffocated me with horror and admiration.

"My eyes were helped by the long half-light of the days
without sun, but they are incapable of distinguishing anything in full light. I shall expect you about the 25th, my little

soul. You will be my inner light and you will guide me through this labyrinth where my life is petrifying little by little, and feels heavy. I'm like a bird to whom they have said, 'you will never be good for anything,' and which bruises itself on everything, not able to believe it."

I do not know whether this honesty about what was happening to her was a conscious act, but she surely had always known (as she wrote to me) that "everything that is free from falsehood is a strength." There was great strength in the way she revealed her moments of despair, strength in being able to speak of them at all, and then a different sort of strength in the charm with which she expressed herself, because through it all, like blood in the veins, it was love that coursed with undiminished splendor and vitality.

And there were still compensatory joys—Blanchette's voice reading aloud, their daily expeditions, arm in arm, to do the errands—although these must have tried Blanchette's patience, for with this weightless weight at her side, and the frequent stops (because, as Jean-Do's sight failed, her fear of dizziness increased), they had to allow more than double the usual time for shopping. Every one of the small daily rites became more precious. What had been the decoration of life became life itself—the arrival of the mailman whom they always called "*le chéri*," coffee in Blanchette's room after the noonday meal, and her single allotted cigarette, the suppers the three created out of a lettuce leaf, a sardine, some cheese, laughing over their clumsiness (for the maid now went home at five), the dozens of small jokes that punctuated every enterprise, such as finding a hat or stick that gremlins had seen fit to hide in some preposterous place. The magic circle was still safely drawn around them; they were still three.

And Jean-Do had not given up her teaching entirely, for on one afternoon a week the group of *fidèles*—former students who were now teachers themselves, or married and with families of their own—gathered as punctually as the stars, to listen to her unforgettable voice reciting the hundreds of poems she knew by heart or speaking to them of a new book Blanchette had just read aloud: "Everything free from falsehood is strength. How strongly I felt this only yesterday again, after you had left, when Blanchette took me into her room to read me the end of that little book (and admirable treasure) 'Portrait d'une Amitié by Vercors. I want so much to put this brochure into your hands, darling. It is impossible to give you an idea of the profound beauty of these things, true, simple, deep, like life itself stripped of all the artifices of art, and which reaches supreme beauty through an exact rendering: *Two* men, *one* sentiment born in an hour, nourished on absence, on absolute trust, on two or three brief meetings where each measures himself against the other among violent disagreements and in a silent communion."

Ten years before her death she had written to me, "O Toby dear, I would so love to be the first of the three to go. What ferocious egotism!" Even this was not to be allowed. For Blanchette slipped away in 1948, "my little Blanchette of yesterday and of fifty years ago," and with her went the daily communion, the daily sharing of all that had meant life. But it is here in the midst of cruel desolation that the spring of imagination, tenderness, and poetry leapt up, alive, from an inexhaustible inner strength. The intensity of her loss made it possible, perhaps, for Jean-Do to begin a new life as a writer—she who had been silent for years—for she learned to dictate, to meditate alone in her darkness, and then to speak for a few minutes or hours to the faithful eyes and hands of one of the *fideles* that recorded the portrait of Blanchette, and the final essays in which she celebrated all that she held most dear.

She did not turn inward to indulge in grief. It seemed as if she were now outward bound, filling the emptiness with a constant imaginative concern and discreet sharing of all the lives around her. One by one, they came, the *fidèles*, the old and young friends, to sit on the low chair, hold her two hands in theirs, and talk of anything and everything: "I am expecting Angèle. It is deliciously springlike outside. The gardener is scraping and getting into order the old paths where I still go stumbling from time to time, and my soul is a marsh full of frogs! Courage fails me a little because the Easter holidays will disperse all the birds who sing to me without cease that they still need me, and what to do? Have you read Colette's *l'Etoile Vesper*, it is a very beautiful and deeper Colette than the others. To be old and without legs to run with enriches her genius which is deep and sad. . . . Here is Angèle to save me from suicide. Laugh at me, my Toby."

However, she was always able to rise to the human moment, to create the old atmosphere of festival, of each meeting as an occasion. She did it in a hundred ways, by having prepared a Japanese print from her collection, or some small precious object as a "surprise"; she did it in the wonderfully amazed and childlike pleasure with which she received a bunch of flowers, burying her nose in roses, and saying, "Ah!" She did it by wearing a special bow at her throat, by the charming way she treated her own disabilities: "I thought I would die this week from the obligation to be intelligent"; and she reacted to the disabilities of others with extreme concern, as when she wrote to a friend, "In any case, you may be sure that your need of rest and your fatigue will be scrupulously respected by 'les Maries' of the Echevinage who will stay as still as paralysed mice. . . . One of them, as a matter of fact (it's me) has no legs to stand on. I had already lost my sight, most of my hearing, and a mouth that can bite—at present you will find me changed from below, as I

already was at the summit (if I may put it so). I venture out
onto the smoothest of sidewalks to try to bring back some life
to these melancholy appendages."

There was no Blanchette to lean on now, and Gaspari was
still teaching, like an old workhorse who goes round and
round and cannot stop and whose patent exhaustion filled her
companion with unspeakable tenderness. For it was clear
that Gaspari must be allowed to die in harness, as she did, in
that last year when there was only one child in the school,
one last "petit Bernard" to love and scold. But she would
come at the end of the day, looking pale and wild to sit beside Jean-Do, and murmur, "I only feel well here, only
beside you." The intimacy between them, which had lived
in the shadow of Blanchette's presence and aura, now came
into its own. And Jean-Do was able to say it, once and for
all, in the portrait of Gaspari she dictated after Gaspari's
death:

"It is three years now since I have had to take leave of
myself, I mean to say that when I look in a mirror I see only
a vague shadow which has no resemblance to me, and which
grows fainter every day.

"I do not know whether others have tried to articulate the
distress this state induces in the heart and the mind. One is
no longer sure of being oneself, nor whether it is worth being
it, when one is no longer able to recognize one's own face.
One feels oneself positively gone astray in something which
other people call the world, the house, a garden, and the
gesture of catching onto whatever is there becomes so
natural that one almost changes one's personality in changing one's stance.

"How can I explain, O Gaspari, that it was you who were
able in this disaster to get me used to all my awkwardnesses,
to all my blunders?—For something irreducibly childlike in

you went on saying to me, while my arm stayed tightly clamped to yours in nervous terror: 'But, for heaven's sake, you see perfectly well that we have turned the corner of the street, you see the green bench perfectly well, and the little house we always love to look at every day at the same time.'

"What was there to answer to that, except each day more patiently, more sadly, more gently too: 'But, Gaspari, you know very well that I cannot see, that I no longer distinguish the color of things.'

"And then you laughed, quite simply, with your absent-minded laugh perfectly adapted to the state of affairs which must at all costs not be allowed to become tragic and unbearable. God himself, and the angels, could not have found a better way to make of me what I had to become: an infirm person who no longer thinks of his infirmities. . . . I walked at your side like a limping child to whom one repeats twenty times: 'Come along, little one, do please try to walk properly,' and that was all."

It seemed unspeakably cruel that even Gaspari was to be taken from her. "I feel like an orphan child and like an animal who wants to speak but whom no one would understand."

This was the last ordeal in the journey Jean Dominique was to make toward her own death; but what she did, the final miracle she performed, and the way she did it, was the supreme achievement of her life. Within it lay the mastered grief and loneliness, the disciplines of a lifetime, the humor, and above all the inextinguishable spring of poetry of which she had written long ago, "Poetry is heroic; it accompanies each one of us in what he hopes to create of most intimately difficult and of absolutely gratuitous." For now she who had always been so reserved, so independent, and so proud became completely dependent on the cherishing of others. As she wrote to my mother, "How tiring it is to pass from the hands of one angel to another. What an exercise for the heart and for the spirit!"

It was necessary that strangers come into the house to live, into its secret intimacies, into its silences so full of memories: "But, my love, I can no longer see anything of our cherry tree in flower (it is magnificent), nothing but Blanchette picking up the cherries the thrush lets fall after having pecked them, and laughing from her whole open throat, and Gaspari is laughing on the white bench and you caress Mouny [the cat] with one long caress from his nose to his tail."

Having lost everything, she now took everything and everyone that came her way into her heart. The strangers who came to live in the house, and to take care of her, soon became a last adventure in friendship. Madame Curvers, "Toulima" as Jean-Do named her, did the cooking; M. Curvers was away at his job all day; their son, Phillippe, and the brown poodle, Presto, were regarded with immense curiosity and delight. I remember with what apprehension I opened the first letters of this period, and with what relief I read, "Presto, the curly brown poodle, becomes exactly what we all needed. Oh, what a terrible disaster that Blanchette did not know him! I have begun to dictate *La Maison*. We still have no servant, but Toulima sings in the kitchen and I play false notes on the piano to exercise my fingers. It makes a rather mad and charming noise. I'm teaching Phillippe to recite poetry. Emma is translating Keats and Shakespeare for me. It is passionately interesting."

And a few days later she wrote, "I think that I am going at last to finish *La Maison*. It is built around the good brown poodle. He loves me and hides so that he can sleep under my bed at night. I am becoming intimate with each of the three Curvers, and Toulima, who is Swiss, is as full of fantasy as one could wish. And I think they love me, and we laugh . . ."

She had learned to touch everyone who came near her with love, pure love that needs both to give and to receive. She was irresistible.

And the atmosphere of the house remained intact. There were always flowers in her rooms; there was always the same sense of entering a world when one pushed open the door and could just make out in the half-dark those walls that flowered on all sides with the opulent roses, gardens, and women's faces under large hats of the impressionist painters, Cross and Van Rhysselberghe and Strebelle, who had been her friends. In each of the two rooms there was a large desk, always filled with letters, papers, books; there were small cosy chairs, many bright pieces of material, shawls, soft silks, small comforting cushions to lean against, and the innumerable lares one found again like old friends—the carved Japanese mouse, the lacquered box covered in butterflies, the inlaid tea caddy from England, and the shelves and shelves of books. Nothing had changed in the seventeen years since she had written to celebrate the finding of a lost button, "a Chinese occasional poem for May":

"A flowered button fell when I shook out the coverlet.
It was a button from the flowered waistcoat of a tired young
  girl.
She herself had fallen on the bed like a sleeping flower.
— Now she has gone, light, flying about the world;
But this button that rolled to my feet when I shook out
  the coverlet,
I caught in my hands and I shall not send to her!

The old Mandarin
Fa-Ti-Ghé"

The outwardness of the last years was certainly tragic, but it was so shot through with imagination, with fantasy, with the extraordinary charm of the being who suffered and enjoyed at its center, that it is hard to think of it as tragic. Out of nothing, Jean Dominique was still making everything, as she had seventy-two years before when she had gone through a period of blindness as a little girl and wrote of herself and her father, "Together they breathed deeply, like people who exaggerate their soul because they have no other riches." Yet she knew. She was never less than honest, less than wholly aware of what was demanded of her, and of what she could give. She wrote to my mother, "Oh dear one! If there were not your letters and May's, and so many marvelous patiences surrounding me, how could I support this emptiness, this horror? But I look under my eyelids at faces and things—and I see the hearts and I understand my misery and my happiness at the same time."

She had quite deliberately, with all the rest that she let go, stripped from herself the awe in which she had always been held. But it was right and fitting that at the very end she had one more sign that she was as Blanchette had written after hearing her lecture fifty years earlier, "a privileged being, unique in the world, a little sacred creature, who soars above all of us, and whom we must admire and venerate without comparing and without judging because she is outside all our measures." For in her last illness it happened that the night nurse became a passionate reader of the poems. And when Marie Closset, that tiny fragile being, lay in the last coma, someone, only lately a stranger, sat by her side, lost in the strength and power of the poet, Jean Dominique:

> "Presse de ma douleur, ô Maître,
> Comme d'un pampre pur et vieux,
> Le vin qui fait plaisir aux dieux!"

Each summer during the last years I was able to come for a month or two, to sit every day in the dark study (the blinds kept closed against the light), to hold those small, light hands in mine, to listen once more to the wonderful voice remembering the poems she and Blanchette had loved to recite, and to translate my books to her, page by page, as they were written. It was, as it had been from the beginning, as if we would never be separated from the long perfect communion we had shared, meeting rarely, but never failing to write at least once a week. "Nous revoilà dans les lettres," she often said, evoking Madame de Sévigné as she might an old friend, any one of the *fidèles* who never left her side.

There were nearly forty years between us, and it is an illusion of youth that time does not matter. Life is more severe than one supposes, and it becomes apparent that one does learn a few things later on that the very young cannot know. We feel for them a special tenderness, because we have learned, or are beginning to learn, the cost of wisdom. Yet in this solitary case, in this one *"ineffable rencontre,"* as Jean-Do called our meeting, time did not seem to operate. Was this because we were both poets, exaggerators of the soul? We met as the people in Fra Angelico's paradise meet, to embrace and to be silent, to talk about everything, above all, to laugh at ourselves. At the end, one of the forms of communication Jean-Do invented when she could no longer write letters was to send postcards, images, the visual metaphor to replace words. So she sent to my mother an Angelico fragment where a Franciscan is being embraced by an angel and wrote on the back, "I have chosen this angel because he knows so well how to kiss." Their arms are folded round each other; their cheeks just touch.

I think of how we used to sit on the little sofa by the window after lunch, how I took off her dark glasses and cleaned them and laid them down, and how she leaned her head, where the blood beat so fast it felt like a bird's, against me, and how then she sometimes fell asleep. I think of the pilgrimages we made—how slowly and with what precau-

tions!—to the formal park a few blocks away, where she
could feel the wind from the great beech trees against her
cheek, and where we could sit silently on a bench, hand in
hand, like people who have reached the end of a journey. I
think of the hours when she recited poems by heart, and especially of one by Francis Jammes which begins,

> "Laisse les nuages blancs passer au soleil.
> Il n'y a que toi, la terre et le ciel.
> Ne pense a presque rien. Douces comme du miel,
> aupres des cressons bleus les brebis viendront boire.
> La fille chantera dans la métairie noire,
> Et sur la terre tiède il tombera des poires."

We thought of almost nothing. The time for the ardent
discussions of Mauriac, Camus, Dostoevski, Katherine Mansfield (about whom she had written so discerningly) were
past. All the words were spoken. "Oh my darling," as she
wrote me, "let us stay together until and after death."

And so we have. It is not yesterday; it is now that I read
the letters that tell me all that I need to know about life,
about love, and that final supreme lesson, how to die: "My
little soul, it is St. Médart and it is not raining! I have dictated two pages to Mariette, then we walked in the Avenue
de Fré to the bench where Gaspari and I always sat last
autumn. O May, the garden is all in order, so neat and so
gently old, green and sweet that it seems to be expecting a
visit from Mabel—and in any case, it is expecting you, the
white bench has come down all by itself from the attic, the
strawberry plants are getting ready to put strawberries in
your mouth, and the thrush is telling a story without beginning or end—."